MW01253837

RIPPLE
EFFECT

Growing your business with
insurance and philanthropy

Jack Bergmans

with Marlena McCarthy

civil sector press

Ripple Effect: Growing your business with insurance and philanthropy

Library and Archives Canada Cataloguing in Publication

Bergmans, Jack, 1960-, author

Ripple Effect: Growing your business with insurance and philanthropy / Jack Bergmans with Marlena McCarthy.

ISBN 978-1-927375-28-0 (paperback)

1. Finance, Personal--Canada. 2. Life insurance--Canada. 3. Estate planning--Canada. 4. Charities--Canada--Finance. I. McCarthy, Marlena, 1959-, author II. Title.

HG179.B46 2015   332.024   C2015-907188-7

Published by Civil Sector Press, A division of The Hilborn Group
Box 86, Station C, Toronto, Ontario, M6J 3M7 Canada
416.345.9403 www.charityinfo.ca

Editors: Lisa MacDonald with Janet Gadeski
Cover Art: John VanDuzer
Interior Design: Cranberryink

To my wife Marlena McCarthy,
who planted the seed
for this book when she said,
"We can't continue to ignore the power of using
insurance to multiply the impact people can
have on the work of their favourite charities.
We must get this information out there,
since it's not being taught anywhere else!"

Acknowledgements

There are several people critical to the creation of this book.

First and foremost, thanks go to our partner Judy Doré, the inspiration for creating Bequest Insurance. In 2011, Judy (an experienced financial advisor and insurance broker) asked us why people don't utilize the power of insurance more often to create super-sized legacy gifts. This simple question led us all down a path that answered this question, unearthed several problems, and then revealed many solutions that are crystallized in this book.

Great appreciation goes to Paul Nazareth whose constant encouragement led the Bequest Insurance team to understand how important our work really is in opening up more effective ways of helping people be as generous as they can by using insurance in creative ways. We also thank Paul for his critical feedback on our manuscript.

Our sincere thanks also go to Judy Doré, Malcolm Burrows, Frances Buczko, and Aneil Gokhale for thoughtful reflections on the manuscript which helped make the book better.

Special appreciation goes out to Sandra Mimic, who shared her thoughts about the manuscript and her own inspirational story of giving a powerful gift of life insurance to her alma mater.

We are grateful to the Canadian Association of Gift Planners for bringing together fundraisers and professional advisors alike in the shared goal of helping people fulfill their philanthropic dreams. The Bequest Insurance team appreciates being embraced by Greater Toronto CAGP members, who generously welcomed us to CAGP and shared their thoughts, challenges, and successes of giving through insurance. Their input and workshops inspired Marlena and I to dig deeper into the topic.

Finally, thanks go to Jim Hilborn of Civil Sector Press for realizing that the world needs a book that clearly explains the complex practice of marrying insurance with philanthropy, and for helping us to get this book into the right hands. Our gratitude also goes to Lisa MacDonald, Kathleen McBride and John VanDuzer for helping to shape, polish and give birth to the book.

Table of contents

INTRODUCTION

How can you really know what happens to your assets after you die?

Helping someone with his or her financial planning is one of the most rewarding jobs anyone can have. You are helping people create and realize their dreams.

Having worked as a financial advisor since 1996, I've learned that everyone is interested in how their money can be managed to improve the quality of life for themselves and their loved ones.

I've also witnessed that when clients are ready to face their own mortality, they start pondering the impact their funds and accumulated assets could have on their heirs.

And most also want to explore a dream of leaving behind a memorable legacy that will have a profound and continuing influence on their community or our world through their support of a meaningful charitable cause.

To help people get to the point of pondering their lasting impact, sometimes you can start with asking a simple question:

"What do you want to happen to your money and other assets after you die?"

Most people don't realize that dying without formal plans — including leaving directions in a Will, or assigning beneficiaries of insurance products — means that all remaining assets will be distributed according to fixed government rules. For example, if the deceased was not survived by a legally married spouse or any children, the estate is divided among the parents, siblings and then closest next of kin, in that descending order of priority (whether the deceased liked them or not) after taxes and other fees are deducted, of course.

This is what most people think their estates will look like:

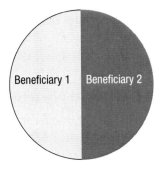

They can't imagine that this is what happens most of the time:

You can help to ensure people realize all of their dreams by being a vital part of your clients' team of professional advisors: financial planners, lawyers and accountants. You can help to guide people towards having enough to live comfortably, and support their loved ones during life and after they're gone. And you can also help them to make caring gifts to support their favourite charitable causes, *enabling people to be a lasting force for positive change*.

As Melinda Gates, Co-Founder and Co-Chair of the transformational Bill and Melinda Gates Foundation, says, "Helping people doesn't have to be an unsound financial strategy."

The immense value you can get out of this book

If you aren't talking to your clients about their big-picture goals, including the lasting positive impact they could have through charitable giving, you are missing out on significant sales opportunities and business-building tools that can create deeper and lasting relationships with your clients, their friends, colleagues and children.

Throughout my training to become a stockbroker, certified financial planner and insurance advisor, I realized that I wasn't being taught how to effectively work philanthropy into my clients' life and estate dreams.

Yet statistics show that 84% of Canadians support charitable causes. The reasons that people support these causes are many, including feeling compassion for others, giving back, and being personally affected by events and circumstances in their lives and in the lives of those around them.

Donors claim that the least popular reason they give to charity is to gain charitable tax credits and pay less tax. As a financial advisor, I have seen how rewarding it is for clients when they know they are having a significant impact on a cause that they really believe in. I've also seen how people are happy to receive charitable tax credits, especially if it means they can leave more to their family.

But deep down, it always made sense for me to ask people about their philanthropic goals while creating their financial plan. This could be partly because I grew up in a family that always gave back, and because I'm married to Marlena McCarthy, whose lifelong career in communications and fundraising focuses on helping people feel good by supporting charities.

Until a few years ago, I hadn't figured out how to best help my clients maximize their giving, while still achieving their lifetime goals and supporting their family. It really was a case of not knowing what I didn't know.

Then in 2011, I became licensed to sell insurance. At that time, Marlena and I talked to a long-time acquaintance Judy Doré, an experienced financial advisor and insurance expert. She shared a question that drove the three of us to form Bequest Insurance and write this book: "I've always helped people make charitable gifts using life insurance and insurance products, which has allowed them to be very generous to their favourite causes. Why don't more people know about this and take advantage of it?"

Today, you have a tool in your hand that will reveal a myriad of ways you can use the powerful tool of insurance to help your clients feel great about their complete financial and estate plan, with the end result being that your business grows, as does your base of referrals.

This book will give you a leg up on many of your competitors, who never bring up charitable giving with their clients and subsequently don't form a deeper bond with them.

Take the next step on your educational journey and learn how to build your business.

Chapter 1

USING INSURANCE
PRODUCTS TO MULTIPLY YOUR CLIENTS' GENEROSITY (AND CUSTOMER LOYALTY!)

"Everyone must leave something behind
when he dies…something your hand touched
some way so your soul has
somewhere to go when you die.
It doesn't matter what you do, so long as you
change something from the way it was
before you touched it into something that's like
you after you take your hands away."

— Author Ray Bradbury in Farenheit 451

A Bequest Insurance client, Frank, approached us in 2014 about making a legacy gift to a small charity he has led and volunteered with for decades.

At age 71, Frank was examining his finances, knowing that he'd have to convert his $42,000 registered retirement savings plan (RRSP) into a registered retirement income fund (RRIF), from which he must withdraw a percentage every year as taxable income. He and his wife knew they didn't need this income to cover present nor future expenses, or provide for their children. They decided to use the annual RRIF income as charitable gifts and if there were any remaining funds, they would gift any residue to the charity in his Will.

Bequest Insurance's financial advisors talked to Frank about his options. If he followed through with his plan, his mandatory RRIF withdrawals (an average of $3,360 a year) would whittle all this money away in twelve and a half years, leaving nothing left to give as a bequest.

Frank asked what would happen if he cashed out his entire RRIF to make a one-time charitable gift. His advisor warned him that this money would all become taxable income and push him into a higher tax bracket, and increase his OAS pension clawback to $6,553 that year. Also, after Frank paid the tax on his RRIF income, he'd only have $29,400 left to donate. Frank quickly dismissed this idea.

Bequest Insurance's financial advisors offered Frank a creative solution that would allow him to leverage his registered savings into a much larger legacy gift for his charity – and cost him nothing to do so. Here's what we did.

We helped Frank make use of an insurance strategy called a "back-to-back" (or insured annuity). First, we helped Frank to purchase an insurance policy that requires premiums to be paid until Frank dies, because it would offer the greatest gift to his charity. To ensure his pre-authorized premium payments are always covered, we moved his $42,000 RRIF into a registered annuity. It generates $3,360 in annual income for life, which is automatically deposited into the same account from which Frank's pre-authorized premium payments are taken.

Frank's annuity income pays for a life insurance policy that is immediately worth $53,000 – an amount that will start to grow after a few years. Frank assigned his charity as the policy's owner and beneficiary, earning him a charitable tax receipt for the $3,360 he pays each year in premium payments. His tax credits eliminate the income tax Frank must pay on his RRIF's annuity income, and also reduces a small amount of income tax on his other income, leaving him with an improved net income each year!

In summary, here's the real beauty of using insurance to give a charitable donation:

Frank turns $42,000 in registered savings into a legacy gift of at least $53,000. After a few years, the value of his policy is likely to grow by a few thousand dollars every year. If Frank lives to 100, his charity could receive at least double the amount of his original investment, and possibly much more. Because this type of donation is outside Frank's estate, it won't be diminished by probate-related fees or taxes.

Frank's policy is guaranteed never to lapse because his annuity income is directly deposited into the chequing account from which his premium payments are automatically withdrawn.

The death benefit from Frank's insurance policy will go to his charity within two to three weeks of the insurance company receiving the insurance claim.

In the end, Frank will be able to offer his charity so much more because he made his gift using insurance, instead of turning his mandatory RRIF deductions into annual donations and assigning any residue to his charity in his Will.

Here is another way to look at what Frank's outcome could be:

Comparing possible outcomes	Frank donates annual RRIF income to charity	Frank buys an annuity and donates a life insurance policy
Frank's annual income	$98,912	$98,912
Annual taxes	($23,021)	($23,021)
OAS clawback	($4,098)	($4,098)
Charitable tax receipt	$3,360/yr for 12.5 yrs	$3,360/yr for life
Net income	$71,793	$71,793
Charity receives	$29,400	$53,000 to $100,000+

Note: These simple changes were incorporated using Frank's existing assets and it costs him nothing. It's new business that helps solidify client relationships and helps fulfill the wishes of leaving a legacy with a greater impact!

So, if helping clients fulfill their goals — including creation of a meaningful charitable legacy — makes clients feel great and thankful to their financial advisors, why aren't more advisors asking their clients about their philanthropic goals?

Chapter 2

INTEGRATING
PHILANTHROPIC GOALS INTO FINANCIAL ESTATE PLANNING

"I realized 10 years ago that
my wealth has to go back to society.
A fortune, the size of which is hard to imagine,
is best not passed on to one's children.
It's not constructive for them."

— Bill Gates, Co-Founder of Microsoft,
Co-Chair of Bill and Melinda Gates Foundation

A 2010 study by Mackenzie Financial showed that only 25% of financial advisors bring up the topic of giving to charity with their clients, and that only 10% of clients initiate the discussion.

Advisors who don't mention philanthropy to their clients give reasons like:

- I'm not trained on how to handle this, so it's beyond my level of expertise; I'll lose the client if I send them to someone else.
- It's none of my business.
- My clients will see this as being "unprofessional". It will lead to a loss of future business.
- It's a topic that is too personal, and is an embarrassing and unnecessary intrusion into my clients' lives.
- If my client gives away their money, my book of business and my income will shrink.

Let's address these specific concerns.

"I'm not trained to handle this."

This book will provide guidance on how to handle philanthropic discussions that was excluded from your formal training. And, we include other sources of information and networking opportunities to help you learn even more.

"It's none of my business/It's too personal/It's unprofessional."

Why would discussing charitable giving be too personal, when typical client discussions cover intensely private topics like births, deaths, marriage, divorce, illness, job loss or promotion, child-rearing and education, retirement planning, religious tithing and more?

A still-relevant 1999 report from the National Centre for

Family Philanthropy (NCFP) a non-profit organization in Washington D.C., concluded that, "Without exception, donors agree that philanthropy is no more personal than any other decisions that advisors help them make. Planning is about all the things you can do with your money. This is one of them. Raising questions of philanthropy does not imply a moral judgment on the advisor's part. It is part of the advisor's responsibility to ask all the questions relevant to a client's interests."

One of the donors polled by the NCFP summed it up nicely:

"Philanthropy should be made an early topic of discussion because it is a fundamental way of achieving some of the outcomes most people would like to achieve."

Let's face it – we can't really present any solutions unless we ask the right questions to uncover our clients' needs and wishes.

"If my client gives away their money, my income will shrink."

On the surface, philanthropy may appear to be a threat to an advisor's business but the results are quite the opposite. In fact, philanthropy can have a significantly positive effect on your business and your client relationships.

What you will gain from discussions including philanthropy

Generate happiness[1]

A survey conducted by the Gallup World Poll between 2006 and 2008 found that in 120 out of 136 countries, people who donated to charity in the past month reported greater satisfaction with life. This relationship emerged in poor and rich countries alike, and across all income groups. Across all 136 countries studied, donating to charity generated happiness

---

1 *Want to Live Long and Prosper? Donate More!* by Kathi Jaworski. Source: Non-Profit Quarterly, Nov. 2011; http://bit.ly/1LEXLtt

equivalent to doubling their household income. (As cited by the Harvard Business School working paper *Prosocial Spending and Well Being: Cross Cultural Evidence for a Psychological Universe.*)

Help clients live longer[2]

Many studies have shown that people who donate their money and time to charity have life expectancies that are 3-10 years longer than those who don't! So by helping your clients fulfill their philanthropic dreams, chances are you'll have them longer as a client, especially for those who give more in relation to the value of their assets.

Increased client retention during financial downturns

Increased loyalty also helps smooth out negative emotions from your clients when markets go down or crash, which is prime time for your competitors to look to poach your clients. With a strong, personal bond to your clients, they are much more likely to trust you with suggestions on how to handle financial downturns, and turn their business over to someone else.

Differentiate, build deeper bonds, increase loyalty, and get referrals

When you can help your clients feel great about their future, which includes the good they are doing by being philanthropic, you create deeper and better financial and emotional relationships with your clients. This will differ from the more simple transactional financial advice of many of your competitors. When you can help your clients find solutions that better meet all of their goals, they are much more likely to give you continuing business, and refer you to their friends and colleagues.

---

2 *Charity Ensures a Longer, Better Life* by Dr. David Lipschitz. Source: creators.com, May 2015. http://bit.ly/20dZbCI

Maintain client relations for generations

Bigger philanthropic decisions are often made on a family basis, due to family members being touched by the same things such as illness that runs in the family, common religious beliefs, or educational institutions and causes that family members have volunteered for and/or supported as a family unit. When you can develop a relationship with client families to help to facilitate gifts that have touched multiple members of the same family, and have creatively arranged for their gift to have the greatest possible effect, you have a better chance of retaining business from younger generations after your client passes away and the intergenerational transfer of wealth occurs.

Build an advisor network and obtain increased professional referrals

In some cases, incorporating philanthropy into planning to achieve multiple client goals can become complex, including having clients create or change their Wills to direct how beneficiaries will receive inheritances, finding more effective ways to give while clients are alive, purchasing life insurance or insurance products, setting up family foundations, or using public trusts or foundations to facilitate donations. Implementing these solutions can involve large or small dollar amounts, and quite frankly may or may not end up being paid work for you.

However, when you engage the other professionals such as accountants and lawyers, that are (or will be) connected to their client's families, you are opening the door to more referrals through these new professional networks. Referrals are the easiest and best ways to grow any business and open doors that otherwise would have been closed to you.

Referral business will continue to grow from within the same families, professional groups and communities that have similar goals and aspirations, which then leads to more referral business, and so on. It's a virtuous cycle and it's good business.

Reduce prospecting time

When business referrals take off, you won't need to spend as much time prospecting for new clients.

Grow your book of business and make your employer happy

Obviously your employer — whether it is an investment or insurance company, bank or credit union — has a vested interest in your success, because they profit from your increased sales and their shareholders demand growth. Make sure you are taking full advantage of any marketing, back-office, product information and product support they offer you.

Fulfill your fiduciary duty

Last but certainly not least, if you are a Canadian financial advisor and avoid the topic of giving to charity with your clients, you may inadvertently be avoiding a part of your basic professional obligations by not doing enough due diligence with them. For more information, read the Investment Funds Institute of Canada's *Fiduciary Duties and Financial Advisors: Frequently Asked Questions and Answers.*[3]

---

3 *Fiduciary Duties and Financial Advisors, Frequently Asked Questions and Answers.* August 2011. http://bit.ly/1GzmNLI

Chapter 3

YOUR CLIENTS
AND CHARITABLE GIVING

"Apart from the ballot box,
philanthropy presents the one opportunity
the individual has to express
his meaningful choice over the direction
in which our society will progress."

— George G. Kirstein,
American publisher and philanthropist

Statistics Canada's Canada Survey of Giving, Volunteering and Participating[4], published in 2013 revealed that 84% of Canadians aged 15 or older make financial donations. The average combined amount individuals give is around $446. That number climbs to 94% if you include gifts of time and goods.

In other words, the vast majority of your clients are *already* charitable in nature, and can benefit from a discussion about their charitable giving.

You may think that getting tax relief is the primary reason that people make donations (more about this in *Chapter 5*). But you couldn't be more wrong.

The Statistics Canada survey also revealed that the most common reasons people give are:

Reasons for making financial donations, donors aged 15 and over

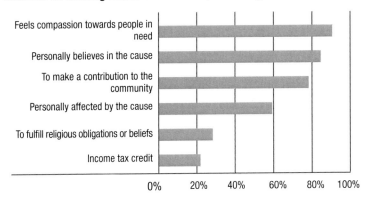

Source: Statistics Canada, Canada Survey of Volunteering Giving and Participating 2007 and 2010.

If you've ever pitched the idea of charitable giving to a client

---

4 *Donors and donations, population aged 15 and over, 2007 and 2010.* Source: Statistics Canada. http://bit.ly/1RCWqVy

based solely on tax-saving ideas, you can understand why many people find the idea distasteful. People give to feel good about doing good!

On the other hand, people do welcome receiving tax credits in exchange for donations. So if you can show that tax savings from charitable giving can help clients achieve other goals, like growing their assets, leaving more to their family, fulfilling their legacy goals, or enhancing their own quality of life, your relationship with them will deepen, and they will value your advice more.

The good news is that Canada's current tax laws are very friendly to charitable donations and we'll explore this in greater depth in *Chapter 5*.

Motivations for larger gifts and bequests are often more profound

People can become introspective when planning to make more significant gifts. They are planning a way to create a powerful, memorable, and lasting legacy by providing support that makes a significant impact on causes close to their heart. As a result, they may want to involve their children and grand-children in gift planning, an exercise that they hope will pass on their values to the younger generations.

The typical bequest in Canada is about $30,000, but a surprising number are in the millions of dollars.

Trends in charitable giving and philosophy are shifting, and it is becoming increasingly important for clients to leave legacy donations to charity rather than leave everything to their kids, especially to those who are already doing well on their own.

As financier and philanthropist Warren Buffet put it: *"I want to give my kids just enough so they would feel they could do anything, but not so much that they would feel like doing nothing."*

Corporate clients and charitable giving

There is a significant amount of charitable giving from Canada's corporate sector. This is done through sponsorships, donations and gifts in kind – around $2.9 billion in 2011.[5]

Although this amount is surprisingly small when compared to charitable giving by individuals ($10.6 billion), it remains a large and viable market for advisors to wade into - particularly in regard to individually or family-owned companies.

Although the owners of small and mid-size corporations often give from the heart to support good causes, there is another powerful underlying motivation. They want to be publicly recognized as being a good corporate citizen, which drives more business.

In fact, the 2010 Global Edelman goodpurpose® study revealed that three out of four Canadians (75%) state they are more likely to give their business to a company that has fair prices and supports a good cause than to a company that provides deep discounts but does not contribute to good causes. More than half said they would switch brands if a brand of a similar quality supported a good cause.

A business will often prefer to give sponsorships, and write off their contribution as a marketing cost. This kind of charitable support does not generate a charitable tax receipt, since the corporation receives a service for their contribution – generous marketing of their support by their charitable partner. This kind of giving is called "cause marketing."

Companies can gain important visibility *and* a charitable tax receipt by making corporate donations, especially when a charity leverages these dollars to generate matching gifts from its donors. The charity pitch is: "We can turn your $1

5 *Tax Incentives for Charitable Giving in Canada* by James Rajotte, MP Chair. Source: Report on the Standing Committee. http://bit.ly/1Nbz9ed

donation into $2 because for a limited time, your donation will be matched dollar for dollar by XYZ corporation. Please give generously." This kind of fundraising appeal is commonly very successful at motivating more individuals to make donations.

According to a study by global management consulting firm McKinsey and Company in 2010, charitable giving can also help family business owners to ensure the longevity of their businesses. This study points out five essential areas of successful family businesses that need to be working well together: family, ownership, business and portfolio governance, wealth management, and charitable foundations.

Regarding foundations, the study says:

Charity is an important element in keeping families committed to the business, by providing meaningful jobs for family members who don't work in it, and by promoting family values as the generations come and go. Sharing wealth in an act of social responsibility also generates good will toward the business…families must cope with the critical challenge of nurturing a consensus on the direction of their philanthropic activities from one generation to the next. Some family foundations have tackled the issue by creating a discretionary spending budget allowing family members to finance projects that interest them. Others give them opportunities to serve on the board or staff of the foundation or to participate directly in philanthropic projects through onsite visits and volunteering schemes. This approach is an especially powerful way to engage the next generation early on.[6]

As a financial advisor working with corporations, it's important that you discuss philanthropic giving with your clients, and realize that tax credits are often not the major driver of corporate giving, just as they aren't with individuals. Rather, they

---

6 *The Five Attributes of Enduring Family Business* by Christian Caspar, Ana Karina Dias, and Heinz-Peter Elstrodt. Source: McKinsey & Company. http://bit.ly/1aNV5sr

are the means by which corporations can increase the value of what they give back to their communities while being seen as good corporate citizens.

It's obvious that using life insurance and other insurance products will amplify the size of charitable gifts and can greatly improve the optics of giving by corporations. This can be a huge bonus for your clients who own corporations.

In some corporate cases, to find the best solutions for your clients you may need to team up with your clients' accountants and lawyers. This will broaden your network of allied professionals, which opens up new business prospects in the future.

The owner(s) of the corporation may wish to give back to the community while they are alive, and also take advantage of insurance products to leave significantly more after they pass away.

You'll learn more about the many benefits of using of life insurance as a tool for charitable giving in *Chapter 6*.

Chapter 4

INTEGRATING
PHILANTHROPY INTO
FINANCIAL PLANNING

"The greatest gift we can give to another
is the purity of our attention."

— Dr. Richard Moss, spiritual coach

To develop a loyal and growing client base, you need to combine the skills you have with the best financial tools available.

You should also explore your own passions and goals, because knowing what matters and what motivates you as a person will help you to better relate to your clients and build deeper relationships.

The more questions you ask of your clients, the more you'll discover that their concerns and objections are really just sign-posts that create focus on what your clients really want to do. These questions are like clearing a path through the woods to help your clients more successfully reach their destination.

Client conversations that dig deeper and produce better results

I've often found that discovering where proper financial advice and a client's emotional needs intersect leads to better and more valuable all-round solutions. Over the years, I've developed many client relationships by exploring ideas with clients in this way. "Mary" and "Sonil" are a composite of many clients.

Mary and Sonil are a married couple. Sonil is semi-retired, working at his long-time employer assembling electronics. Mary retired from teaching a few years ago. The purpose of our meeting was to review the strength of their financial situation and determine if they could live a life free of financial worries if Sonil fully retired.

Here are a few thoughts that were going through my head at the beginning of the conversation.

There's a lot more to financial planning than just seeing where the money goes and determining whether this couple can save more. Looking at income, savings and expenses is a good start to get baseline solutions because numbers don't lie. But this clinical approach isn't enough. I must learn this couple's priorities.

I have to keep in mind that for most people saving is a lower priority because they know they only live once. Yes, we have to figure out how the bills get paid, but I've got to look for the intersection between the financial resources these people have and how they prioritize how they're going to use those resources.

A standard risk assessment questionnaire doesn't go far enough, and doesn't even bring up more serious conversations like charitable giving, which can deepen my relationship with the couple, and likely open up additional revenue streams for me as a result.

I learn that Mary and Sonil have a comfortable life they're very happy with. Both have hobbies and interests that fit into their budget or have a negligible effect on it. Both sing with their church choir, and afterwards, socialize with the group at a local pub. They have a weekly date night at a restaurant, and often entertain friends at their home. In warm weather, Mary golfs every Saturday with old college friends. And during the winter, Sonil plays goalie in a hockey "beer league." Every year, during the depths of Toronto's winter, they go someplace warm for a few weeks.

Their two sons have given them three grown grandkids. All are "upwardly mobile," so the couple doesn't spend money buying them trinkets any longer. They get more out of spending time with them.

Mary and Sonil's accumulated savings amount to about three years of their combined pre-tax income. Now that the kids are gone, they are saving more than ever. They have a common aversion to downward fluctuation in the value of the investments they're depending on to fund their retirement. Beyond the money they regularly call upon to meet current needs, they don't mind if the value of their other investments fluctuate as long as the value is expected to recover in short order from down cycles. I helped them make a few small adjustments to their portfolio to address this concern.

The couple owns their home, and their expenses, including insurance, heat, electricity and property taxes, are relatively fixed. On the advice of Mary's dad, they didn't buy mortgage insurance through their bank when they bought their house, but purchased term insurance on themselves to cover mortgage payments should anything happen. When their incomes allowed, they converted their term insurance to permanent policies repurposed to cover income and any additional expenses when one predeceases the other.

They felt they needed disability and long-term care insurance because they don't want to become a burden on their two kids, so I helped them find the most appropriate policy at the best price.

Financially, their kids are doing "just fine," so they feel it's no longer necessary for them to be the primary beneficiaries of their estate. This opened a conversation about what is important to them. They talk about wanting to give back to their community, and have done so for years by volunteering at a local community centre.

Their interest stemmed from their experience with their older son, Anil, who kept getting into trouble during his teens – break and enters, minor property damage, and petty thefts. He was turned around by a local after-school program that is still run out of the same community centre. They are proud that Anil is now a good father, a foreman in a large construction company, and a volunteer baseball and hockey coach, also at the community centre.

Both Sonil and Mary are grateful for what that centre does for kids, and want it to continue to thrive when they can no longer be a part of it. They make annual donations and have considered making a large gift, but feel that this might have more impact after they are gone, when their gifts of time and money stop.

I also learned that their registered plans would soon be generating an annual income stream that will put them into a higher tax bracket.

Now I had a framework to create a cost-effective and simple solution to help them finance their retirement, lower their taxes, and generously support their favourite charity.

After exploring a number of solutions, we settled on this:

To take care of their legacy gift, I suggested that Sonil, who is in good enough health, purchase a life insurance policy, and name the community centre to be its owner and beneficiary. By doing this, his annual premiums become charitable donations, for which the community centre provides charitable tax receipts.

Once I had confirmation that Sonil was approved for life insurance, I suggested a guaranteed way to cover his premiums. We transferred some of his registered savings from their local bank's guaranteed income certificates into an annuity with an insurance company, which is giving him a much higher guaranteed income for life than the minimum payments he'd be required to deduct from his registered plan. He uses some of that income to pay the annual premiums on his life insurance policy, and the tax credits he receives for the premiums more than cover the tax payable on the annuity payments.

An interesting trend that I've been encountering is an increase in the number of people wanting to see their donations make a difference while they are alive. This tracks very nicely with current financial plans, reducing current taxes, and good estate planning to reduce potential estate taxes owing. This is a terrific opportunity for financial advisors to add even more value to their clients, deepen your relationships with them, and open up new income opportunities for you.

By offering your clients creative solutions that, if appropriate, include annuities, life insurance and other insurance investments, you could help them increase their take-home income, decrease their taxes, and create larger and more meaningful legacies for their family and favourite charitable causes. When this happens, increased referrals will drive your business to new levels.

In addition, you'll be making your boss happy and setting yourself up to be promoted, or perhaps to become the replacement for your boss!

Of course, many would say that integrating philanthropy into your life and work is simply good karma.

Seven important topics in philanthropy

To help you unearth clients who will welcome discussions about philanthropy, it is helpful to deepen your knowledge of philanthropy and charitable giving. Some of these topics are covered here, and you'll find more great information in some of the books we recommend towards the end of this book:

1. **Discover what charitable giving options exist.** *Planned Giving for Canadians* is a Bible on estate giving of all sorts. For other powerful educational resources, see *Chapter 10.*

2. **Being aware of current challenges and successes in the fundraising world is a significant differentiator for financial advisors.** Becoming a member of the Canadian Association of Gift Planners (CAGP), and attending their educational workshops and conferences is an easy way to

keep up with ongoing industry trends and is a significant educational and networking tool.

3. **How to spot the points of intersection between smart financial planning and philanthropy.** For example, charitable tax breaks can allow individuals to better care for their loved ones after they are gone. You can also find ways to ensure your client's charitable aspirations are fulfilled and can be amplified to achieve even better outcomes. You can help clients who are business owners create customer loyalty and expand their customer base. And, you can help owners ensure the longevity of personal corporations.

4. **How your clients can give more to charity with the same money.** Life insurance and insurance products are often the best and easiest tools available to provide that opportunity. More examples of this to follow.

5. **How to keep money in the hands of your clients, during life and after death.** This can include strategies that reduce the size of estates and encourage more charitable giving during life. A deeper look into charitable tax receipting in Canada in *Chapter 5* also demonstrates some advantages that aren't typically well understood.

6. **How clients can pass on their values and strengthen family bonds by engaging loved ones in charitable giving decisions.** This is described in more detail in a summary of a McKinsey and Company study in *Chapter 3*.

7. **How to choose between giving to charity or giving to the taxman.** The concept of choosing to give money to charity rather than to the taxman is an idea that intrigues clients. This idea can be used as a hook to discuss ways they can take advantage of insurance products, often opening up new business for you. Clients particularly like learning ways insurance products can help them leverage a larger charitable

gift, without any additional capital outlay on their part.

How to identify clients who are interested in charitable giving

On average, 84% of Canadians 15 and older (or just under 24 million people) reported making at least one financial donation to a charitable or nonprofit organization. This number climbs to 94% if you include gifts of material goods or food. So it's not hard to find people interested in philanthropy. However, here are some examples of people who would be most keenly interested:

- **Thrifty people** who like the idea of their donation being significantly multiplied, and/or those looking for ways to lower their annual or estate taxes. Similarly, people who would rather give back than give to the taxman.

- **Females** give slightly more than men.

- People with **higher incomes and levels of education**.

- **Those who volunteer** their time to charities – especially those on boards of directors.

- People who are **religiously active**.

- **Detail-oriented planners.**

- **Parents** concerned their children might challenge a traditional bequest in an attempt to gain a larger inheritance.

- **Affluent parents** who are concerned that bequeathing all their wealth to their children will tempt the kids to do nothing with their lives.

- **Childless individuals/couples** who have done well financially, or whose children are well off or have predeceased them. This includes gay and lesbian individuals and couples, older women who have never married and who prefer the title "Miss", and people with no other heirs.

- People who want to **make their executor's job easier**.

- People in their **peak earning years**. Middle to upper income individuals, 40-55 years old, who are largely debt-free, with very good cash flow. Those who have done very well in their careers or have come into significant money at a younger age.

- **People who have received a large inheritance, business gain or windfall.** Large windfalls can result in large tax bills that can be offset by charitable donations.

- **Older individuals** who have experienced the death of parents, family or friends, have come to terms with their own mortality, and want to put their affairs in order.

- **Family-focused** people who want to be very philanthropic, but are reluctant to leave money through their Will because it will erode the value of their estate and force them to leave less to their family.

- **Financial advisors, insurance agents or brokers, and accountants**. Yes, this kind of giving can work well for you, too! These individuals are more likely to understand the tax and personal benefits of incorporating philanthropy in financial and estate planning.

Charitable Giving By Canadians[7], a 2012 Statistics Canada study by Martin Turcotte, is an excellent resource to learn more about who constitutes a typical Canadian donor and motivates them to give.

Leveraging the power of insurance, and youth, to create a legacy with powerful and lasting impact

Here's the story of Sandra Mimic, financial advisor/insurance broker turned major and planned giving fundraiser, who worked two insurance gifts into her legacy plans.

---

7 *Charitable Giving by Canadians* by Martin Turcotte. Source: Statistics Canada. http://bit.ly/1RgXQFe

Using insurance for charitable giving is often something older people consider, but for people in their 20s, 30s and 40s, their youth can offer them the chance to make an affordable donation today that can grow exponentially in size over their lifetime.

Sandra Mimic has used insurance in two different ways to create a lasting legacy for two organizations close to her heart.

When she was 35, Sandra — a successful financial advisor and insurance specialist — gave her first charitable gift of life insurance to her university, which had had a profound effect on her life.

Her university invited her to make a charitable gift to help endow a new student bursary fund that would generate annual bursaries to future students attending her campus. Wanting future students in need to have access to the same great education she received, she agreed.

Drawing on her financial background, she began to consider her own circumstances to determine what kind of gift would give her the most bang for her buck.

At age 35 in 2005, Sandra was raising a family and had a large mortgage.

She had recently purchased insurance to protect her family, and she began to explore using insurance to make her gift.

Being a licensed insurance broker, she did a quote on herself. As a healthy non-smoker, she calculated that she could afford a $50,000 30-pay policy with $30-a-month premiums.

Sandra then worked out the logistics of the gift with the university's planned giving fundraiser. Because Sandra was giving the policy's ownership to the university, they signed an agreement with Sandra to accept the policy. They also signed off on Sandra's policy application, and got a written assurance from her that she agreed to continue paying all the premiums. Sandra provided them with written instructions to designate the policy's proceeds to the student bursary fund, as she had discussed with the university's fundraiser.

Because the university owns Sandra's policy, they send Sandra one charitable tax receipt each year for her total annual premium payments. The tax credits generated by the charitable tax receipts reduce Sandra's real monthly premium cost to about $18.

Says Sandra, "Making a gift using life insurance was a no-brainer. In the end, it will cost me about $6,400 to give a gift of $50,000. I also enjoy staying connected to the university by being one of their Legacy Society members."

As a financial advisor, Sandra made a point of talking to her clients about their philanthropic goals, because she personally understands how personally fulfilling it is to include charitable giving into life planning.

This understanding later led Sandra to switch careers, and become a planned giving fundraiser for her university.

Today, Sandra fulfills the wishes of children with life-threatening illnesses in her role as Major and Planned Giving Officer for The Children's Wish Foundation of Canada. She decided to leave a legacy to Children's Wish by using insurance in a different way.

"My employee benefits include group life insurance coverage. Since I already have lots of life insurance to protect my family, I named Children's Wish to be the beneficiary of my group insurance. If I leave this position, I can convert the insurance into permanent insurance to ensure I'll continue to fulfilling children's wishes after I've passed away."

Sandra reflects, "As a financial advisor, I loved helping my clients meet both their financial and philanthropic goals. As a fundraiser, my heart is touched every day as I help donors' spirits soar through carefully planned donations that brighten the lives of children with serious and life-threatening illnesses."

....

Effective conversation starters

Sometimes the concepts and ideas of giving to charity and philanthropy in general haven't fully formed, or people limit their thinking of charitable giving based on their immediate cash flow or just the amount of money they have in their pockets today.

In other cases, people may be quite charitable, already giving regularly to charity, and having included charitable giving in their estate planning.

You usually can't tell if someone is charitably minded just by looking at them so the easiest way to find out is to ask. There's no 'best way' to introduce charitable giving – there are as many ways to approach the topic of charitable giving as there are people.

Here are six ways you can ease into the topic. I'm sure you'll find some ideas that are comfortable for you.

1. **For anyone:** "Would you be interested in learning about some financial strategies that will cost you nothing and that will allow you to leave more to both your loved ones and your favourite charities?"

2. **For those reluctant to create a Will or think of future planning:** "What do you want to happen to your money and other stuff after you die?" It may well be they don't know what happens when people have not formally planned ahead, and don't realize that a lack of planning is likely to result in their assets not going where they want them to. Insurance products can be highly beneficial for this kind of client, since assets in insurance investments can

allow clients to remain in control of these funds during their lifetime. It will also allow them to pass these assets to their beneficiaries outside their estate. That offers many benefits including making gift-giving private, lowering taxes, and decreasing the hassle on the executor and their beneficiaries. None of these outcomes are experienced by people whose investments are held outside an insurance company.

3. **For those with excess capital:** "Is leaving a charitable legacy something that you've given thought to? What would that look like? Can you see involving your children in planning this charitable legacy?"

4. **For those who hate paying taxes:** "Would you be interested in learning about some cost-free ways to save you money on taxes and help you to give more to your favourite charities and your loved ones?"

5. **For those interested in leaving a legacy:** "After you're gone, how would you like to be remembered?" People who like to lead by example are often keen to leave behind a meaningful legacy.

6. **For religious people:** "Are there programs at your place of worship that you would like to support, either now or through a memorable charitable legacy gift?"

7. **For those concerned that taxes will diminish what they can leave to loved ones:** "If you're worried you'll be able to leave less to loved ones because of taxes that will be due against your estate, many of our clients like to reduce their taxes by making a gift to their favourite charity. An easy way to imagine how you can do this is to include a division of your estate to go to charity, just as if it were another child to take care of."

Retired Canadian fundraiser Helen DeBoer championed the **Charity Child** concept for people who are concerned that taxes will significantly decrease what they can leave to loved ones. She explains that by making a philanthropic bequest to a "charity child" in a Will, people can both have a lasting impact on causes they believe in, and use the charitable tax credits to offset estate taxes and leave more to family and friends.

Division of Estate

This story illustrates one way to use insurance to make her strategy work.

Rajesh and Myrna, both 65, expected to pass their cash assets and house to their only son Peter (and his wife and their twin one-year-olds) through their Wills.

The value of their cash and investment assets was easy to calculate. But when their neighbour's house sold for $1.2 million, they realized that Peter and his wife, who both had successful careers, would inherit much more than they'd ever imagined. They recognized that they could afford to both support Peter and his family, *and leave a generous gift to their favourite charity, which their advisor affectionately called their "charity child."*

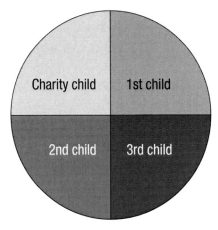

Their financial advisor helped Rajesh and Myrna calculate what kind of money they needed to finance their retirement, and as a safety net to cover future health care costs.

Next, the couple decided to leave the value of their house (which Peter had no interest in moving into) to their son. To his twins, they had planned to leave each of them $20,000 in their Will.

The couple also had about $115,000 in investment assets that could make a generous legacy gift to a "charity child." Their first instinct was to name a charity in their Will to receive these funds, which were growing in value each year. Keeping all of this in mind, their advisor suggested making a number of changes that would allow Rajesh and Myrna to pay less to give more, decrease the size and complexity of their estate, pay less tax, and make the executor's job much simpler. First, the couple used life insurance, backed up by annuities, to support their grandkids and a "charity child."

Myrna and Rajesh were thrilled to learn that they could take $33,823 from their investment assets to buy a 20-year term annuity. The annuity payments would completely fund *two* $100,000+ policies. So instead of leaving their grandchildren bequests of $20,000 each, the couple purchased a $100,000 *participating life insurance policy* on the life of each of their grandchildren. This kind of policy offers life insurance with a growing death benefit, and competitive cash value growth resulting from reinvested annual dividends provided by the policy. The twins could begin to access the cash value once they reached the age of majority (18). With the bequest to the twins made in this way, the kids have access to cash values they can use throughout their life. They may use it to pay for their education, a down payment on a house, to start a business, and or even use this growing asset to generously support their own kids and a "charity child" of their own when they pass away.

To make their charitable gift, Myrna used the balance (about

$80,000) of their investment asset to buy another annuity that cover the premiums on a $100,000 life insurance policy based on her own life. On this policy, she named their favourite charity as its beneficiary.

Had Myrna and Rajesh supported their "charity child" through one of their Wills, their gift would have taken about a year to get to their charity, after their entire estate cleared probate, and after income tax, legal and executor fees were paid.

By donating the death benefit of an insurance policy, Myrna removes her gift from her estate which will reduce her probate taxes. Even better, her gift will be forwarded to their charity within only two to three weeks of her executor filing a claim with her insurance company.

Either way Myrna makes her donation, her estate will receive a charitable tax receipt for the entire value of her gift. However, she chose a life insurance policy that will grow over her lifetime, which will generate a larger donation and a higher tax receipt that may completely eliminate her taxes!

Myrna's smile was even bigger when she learned that buying an $80,000, 20-year term annuity would cover all her premiums, and if she lived to age 85, her charity would receive a benefit of about $147,000!

You can see the many advantages of this strategy in the following chart:

Original financial plan	Revised plan using insurance
Grandchildren's inheritance (before)	**Grandchildren's inheritance (after)**
$20,000 (cash) x2 = **$40,000**	**A $100,000 participating life insurance policy** for each child, with growing cash value & death benefit Cash value of policies when twins reach 18: **~$32,000 x 2 = $46,000** + death benefit at age 18: **~$132,268** (and growing) **x 2 = $264,536** For heirs of the twins and their favourite charities
Estate taxes & probate-related fees & taxes, and reduction of bequests to other beneficiaries = **($4,800)**	Estate taxes & probate-related fees & taxes = **$0** (Bequest to twins occurs outside of the estate)
Cost of these bequest to the estate: = **($44,800)**	Cost of 20-year term annuity to fund all premiums on two $100,000 policies = **($33,823)**
Total inheritance remaining after taxes and fees = **$40,000**	Total inheritance = **$310,536** (likely much more)
Inheritance received about one year after death of grandparents (after probate on whole estate is settled)	• **Access to growing cash value when twins turn 18** • **Death benefit** will grow throughout twins' lives and will be **delivered to their heirs and charities within 2-3 weeks** of filing insurance claim
Charitable gift (before)	**Charitable gift (after: "Charity Child")**
Gift from will $100,000 (cash)	**Gift of $100,000 life insurance policy** Value if Myrna lives to 85: = $146,721
Estate & probate-related fees & taxes owing on $100,000 held within the estate = **($12,000)**	Estate & probate-related fees & taxes – not applicable since donation of life insurance benefit occurs outside of the estate = **$0**
Total donation = **$100,000**	Total donation = **$146,721**
Charity receives donation after probate is settled (**about one year later**)	Charity receives donation within **2-3 weeks** of executor filing of insurance claim
Cost to the estate = **($112,000)**	Cost of 20-year term annuity to fund policy = **($80,000)**
Tax credits from donation = **$88,000**	Tax credits from donation = **$146,721**

Chapter 5

UNDERSTANDING
CANADIAN CHARITABLE
TAX CREDITS

"I've always respected those
who tried to change the world for the better,
rather than just complain about it."

— Michael Bloomberg, former Mayor of New York City,
Business Magnate, Philanthropist

In Canada, the legislation surrounding the reimbursement for charitable donations through federal and provincial tax credits is more generous than it has ever been. The government rewards charitable giving because charitable organizations provide a wealth of vital services that the government could not implement as effectively, nor pay for through taxes alone.

At its most basic level, the legislation allows Canadians to offset up to 75% of their annual income taxes owing, using charitable tax credits. Spouses can combine their credits and use them on the income tax return that provides the best tax advantage.

Tax credits in excess of the 75% limit can be carried forward and used against taxes in any of the next five subsequent years.

After the donor passes away, charitable tax credits can offset 100% of estate taxes for the final year. If the donation tax credit exceeds the final year's taxes, an executor can claim the balance against income tax paid in the year previous to death.

Legislation from Canadian Bill C43 (effective as of January 1, 2016) introduced positive changes on how estates can handle charitable gifts through the Will. These gifts can be attributed for charitable tax receipt purposes to the final tax return, previous tax year, or to any of the first three years of the estate, which is now called a Graduated Rate Estate (GRE). Beyond this 3-year period, an estate may forfeit the use of valuable charitable tax receipts if they have not yet been claimed.[8]

These legislative changes may create opportunities to start discussions with clients surrounding the intentions they already have documented in their existing Wills. Depending on client circumstances, it may be prudent to discuss making changes to ensure that intended charitable gifts flow outside of the estate. Directing charitable beneficiaries on insurance products

8 *Graduated Rate Estates (New Changes in Bill C-43)* by Victoria L. Hockley. Source: Miller Thomson. http://bit.ly/21zbsCA

can accomplish this. Insurance can also be used to cover the potential loss of use of charitable tax receipts by the estate.

Charitable tax credits are not progressive or reliant on a person's level of income, unlike tax brackets. A portion of the tax credit comes from the federal government and the balance comes from the home province or territory of the taxpayer. The federal charitable tax credits are consistent for every Canadian. Yet each province and territory provides different charitable tax credits.

There is a lower percentage of both federal and provincial tax credit on the first $200 of charitable donations made within a calendar year, and a higher percentage on both tax credits for any donations over $200.

Online charitable donation tax calculator:
Source: Canada Revnue Agency. http://bit.ly/1fAyPlz

Example: How a simple monetary charitable donation works

This example comes from the Canadian Revenue Agency's website:

Danielle lives in the province of Saskatchewan and donated $400 in 2013 to registered charities.

1. The federal charitable tax credit rate is 15% on the first $200 and 29% on the remaining $200. Her federal tax credit is therefore (15% × $200) + (29% × 200) = $88.

2. The provincial charitable tax credit rates for Saskatchewan for 2013 are 11% on the first $200 and 15% on the remaining $200. Therefore her provincial tax credit is (11% × $200) + (15% × $200) = $52.

3. Her combined charitable tax credit is ($88 + $52) = $140. $140 is a tax credit for 35% of her donation.

Charitable Tax Credit on $400 donation (Saskatchewan)

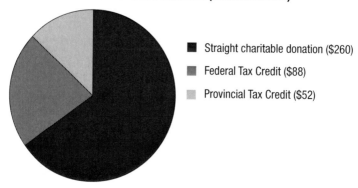

- Straight charitable donation ($260)
- Federal Tax Credit ($88)
- Provincial Tax Credit ($52)

When people start to make larger gifts, the lower tax credit on their first $200 in donations becomes virtually insignificant. In general, generous Canadians will receive combined tax credits from 40 to 50 percent of the value of their gifts, depending on the province or territory in which they live.

Charitable Tax Credit on $2000 donation (Saskatchewan)

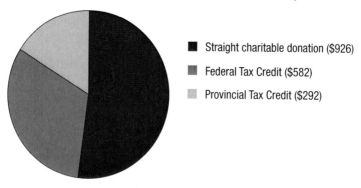

- Straight charitable donation ($926)
- Federal Tax Credit ($582)
- Provincial Tax Credit ($292)

Special charitable tax credits

First-time donor super credit

A temporary donor super credit provides an extra 25 percent federal credit on top of the original charitable donation tax receipt.

Canadians are considered first-time donors if neither they nor their spouse or common-law partner have claimed and been allowed a charitable donations tax credit for any year after 2007. The credit only applies to a gift of money — a maximum of $1,000 made in one taxation year — made between March 21, 2013 and 2017. It can only be claimed once.

This means that eligible donors can get a 40 percent federal credit for monetary donations of $200 or less, and a 54 percent federal credit for the portion of the donations that are over $200, to a maximum of $1,000. The donation also qualifies for the regular amount of provincial or territorial tax credit.

Donations of publicly traded shares and stock options

Capital gains taxes are completely eliminated when a Canadian donates appreciated public traded shares or stock options directly to a registered charity. The tax credit is not available if a person sells their stocks and donates cash equivalent to their value to a charity. The charitable tax receipt will be based on the value of the shares or stock options on the day they are donated to the charity.

There are other types of capital property to which this donation credit applies. To learn more, visit the Canadian Revenue Agency's website: http://bit.ly/1PXtHwi

Donations of registered savings

The two most effective ways to make donations from the proceeds of an RRSP or a RRIF are through estate gifts:

1. Donors can name their favourite charity as the designated beneficiary of their plan. They would do so by registering this change with the trustee of their plan.
    or

2. Donors can bequeath the proceeds of their RRSP or RRIF

to their favourite charity through their Will.

In both cases, their charity will issue a charitable tax receipt to their estate. This helps the estate to offset or eliminate the taxes that will be due on the RRSP or RRIF.

By naming any registered charity as beneficiary of an RRSP or RRIF, the charity becomes the direct recipient of the entire value of the funds, which are not required to go through probate because of the beneficiary designation, and may be protected from possible creditor claims against the estate. Note: although registered accounts with a proper designated beneficiary are technically not required to go through probate and the values are not included for probate tax purposes, most non-insurance financial institutions will not release these assets to an executor without first having received a notarized copy of the letters of probate.

It should be noted that general tax rules and laws are set by the Canadian Revenue Agency and provincial governments. It is not unusual for tax laws to change from one government budget to the next.

For example, a 2014 federal proposal changed how charitable donations from estates are handled, starting January 1, 2016. The executor of a typical estate, called a Graduated Rate Estate or GRE, now has the flexibility to allocate the tax credits generated by a donation designated in a Will, or any donation made by the estate 36 months after death, to:

- the tax year of the estate when the donation is made; or
- an early taxation year of the estate; or
- the final two tax years of the deceased person.

For more information on Bill C-43 the law offices of Miller Thomson offer further information. http://bit.ly/1Rqid4Y

You can also visit the Miller Thomson website. Their monthly online Charities and Not-for-Profit Newsletter offers careful analysis of the ever-changing Canadian charitable tax landscape. http://bit.ly/1f7n86Q

To keep track of current tax law, visit the CRA website: http://bit.ly/1B9XZCS

Chapter 6

USING INSURANCE
TO FULFILL CLIENT GOALS AND LEAVE BEHIND A MEANINGFUL LEGACY

"My father used to say,
'You can spend a lot of time making money.
The tough time comes when you have
to give it away properly.'
How to give something back –
that's the tough part in life."

— Lee Iacocca, former Chairman of Chrysler and Ford,
Philanthropist

When you have a good understanding of all of the goals your clients wish to achieve — including having enough money to last them to their final days, supporting their family, and fulfilling a philanthropic dream — it is very rewarding when you can help people do more with what they have by simply rearranging how they hold their assets.

There are many ways you can make this happen for your clients by including life insurance and insurance products into their asset mix. I'm not suggesting that you immediately start selling your clients on any particular insurance products. Instead, keep them in mind while presenting overall solutions to allow clients to do more of what they want to do.

Here's an excellent example of integrating insurance and adding new business to your practice that results in very happy and loyal clients.

. . . .

Mike and Samantha, Ontarians and both aged 65, are healthy and happily retired. They live comfortably, thanks to both having good employee pensions, money in tax-free savings accounts (TFSAs), and several investments including about $350,000 in RRSPs. They have only two main legacy goals:

- After they are gone, they want to generously provide for their daughter Jane, who has four children;
- They want to leave a generous legacy gift to the university where they met, and that they both attended.

Through their Wills, they have designated their daughter to receive whatever remains in their registered funds (RRSPs/RRIFs) when they die. Because they don't live extravagantly and have other sources of income, they only take out the minimum required deductions from their registered savings. They do want to leave a generous amount to Jane, but are concerned that income taxes and probate-related fees and taxes will consume about half of their registered savings, before the residue goes to Jane.

They have also assigned a $75,000 bequest to their university, which they have set aside in TFSAs. The spouse that passes away last will make the donation.

You realize that there are more effective ways for them to meet their goals. After working through various options, you realize the best is to make some no-cost changes that will allow Mike and Samantha to be much more generous to both their daughter and their university.

You advise the couple to take their $75,000 in the TFSAs, and with it buy a $300,000 Universal Life joint-last-to-die life insurance policy, assigning Jane as its beneficiary.

Sam and Mike then go to their lawyer and update their Wills, removing the $75,000 bequest to their university. On your advice, they replace it with a donation of the proceeds of their registered savings funds, which are allowed to transfer to their university upon their death.

Mike and Samantha pass away 20 years later. Because of their pension and investment income, they were able to stick to only making the minimum required withdrawals from their registered savings, which are worth $200,000. The entire amount goes to their university – instead of the $75,000 they had originally planned to give.

It is true that their estate will owe income taxes on these funds, but they are completely offset by the $82,000 charitable receipt their estate receives for their generous gift.

Their daughter Jane immediately receives the full tax-free death benefit of her parents' insurance policy, now worth about $378,000 – instead of about $120,000 that would have resulted from the transfer of the RRSP residue, after taxes and probate were settled.

Original finanicial plan	Revised plan using insurance
Charitable gift	**Charitable gift**
$75,000 from TFSA	**$200,000** from RRIFs
+ Tax credits from donation $30,750	- income tax owed on RRIFs ($82,000)
	+ Tax credits from donation $82,000
Daughter's inheritance	**Daughter's inheritance**
Balance of RRIF $200,000	Insurance policy death benefit **$378,000**
Minus taxes and probate-related fees and taxes: ($82,000 + $4,500)	*Taxes and probate-related fees and taxes - not applicable*
Total inheritance **$113,500** received after probate is settled (**about 9 months later**)	Total inheritance **$378,000** received within **2-3 weeks** of insurance company receiving parent's death certificate

Note: The amount of insurance purchased for $75,000 will vary according to the age and health each individual being insured. The value of registered funds upon death of their owners will vary from Canadian province to province due to different tax rates (and probate-related fees and taxes, for registered funds that are not designated as charitable donations).

How life insurance and insurance products can fulfill multiple client needs

In general, most of your clients will have a similar hierarchy of needs when it comes to their financial and estate plans. The order and magnitude may be somewhat different, yet people generally like to be sure of four things:

1. Financially taking care of their family

2. Financially taking care of themselves

3. Supporting their place of worship

4. Fulfilling a philanthropic goal of giving back to society or leaving the world a better place.

How much, in what order and when are the primary questions and the answers often become a simple question of math. Those who may need to use their capital during their lifetimes are often best to leave any residual values to beneficiaries – both family and charities. For those with excess capital, who can take care of their families and themselves, it becomes a question of timing. "Do we support my kids and charities now? Later? Take care of them through our Wills? Or a combination of all the above?"

Of course, one of the first things to consider in making client dreams come true is to find ways to lessen their tax liability, during life and after they're gone. Even though most clients' primary focus when considering donations isn't taxes, I've been able to help many people do much more with what they have by taking advantage of charitable tax credits.

Life insurance is a great tool, and I'll help you understand the many ways you can use it and other insurance products to make donations, and help clients in many other ways.

You should also keep in mind other highly beneficial special tax credits on first time gifts, appreciated public stocks, and registered savings mentioned in *Chapter 5* that can help magnify donations and family support, like Mike and Samantha were able to do.

A short primer on insurance products

These are the most commonly used insurance products that you should keep in mind when structuring your clients' finances to meet their goals.

Life Insurance

The concept of pooling allows people to significantly multiply the value of their intended charitable gifts. The benefits flow to beneficiaries tax-free.

For those who want to give large donations during their lifetime, life insurance can also be used as a wealth replacement tool to keep the value of estates whole and ensure clients can also leave more for all of their beneficiaries.

Annuities

People provide a lump sum to an insurance company to purchase an annuity, which then guarantees an income stream for life. This can help ease the fear of many clients that they'll run out of money before they die. Annuities also usually offer a higher income stream than other guaranteed sources of income like GICs and government bonds. They are also often much more tax friendly in non-registered accounts, which leaves more money in your clients' pockets than they would have had otherwise.

Annuities come with the choice of a guarantee periods from 0 up to 20 years during which any residual value from the initial lump sum invested will go to named beneficiaries outside of the Will and the estate.

Annuities can include inflation protection. Being a different asset class, they can also help to diversify your clients' portfolios.

Annuities can facilitate larger insurance legacy donations by being used to fund the premiums on life insurance policies whose beneficiary and/or ownership is assigned to a charity.

Prescribed annuities are remarkably tax-friendly when held outside of registered accounts. After-tax income is higher in comparison to most other guaranteed investment classes. The increased net income opens the door to additional investment options and/or higher annual charitable donations that offer further tax relief. It's a virtuous cycle. The low taxation of income from prescribed annuities also significantly lowers the risk of claw-back on income-tested government pensions and other benefits including Old Age Security, Guaranteed Income Supplements, and tax deductions for expenses related to long-term care, caregivers and medical costs.

Variable annuities (also known as Guaranteed Minimum Withdrawal Benefit plans or GMWBs) are often used for retirement income because they offer guaranteed minimum payments for life. Funds placed in variable annuities are invested in a portfolio of segregated funds; if investment performance exceeds the minimum contractual guarantees, annuity payments permanently increase in size. Billions of Canadian dollars are invested in these variable annuities, so your client can be philanthropic by assigning their charity as the beneficiary to receive any residual value remaining in the variable annuity upon the client's death.

Some larger charities offer charitable gift annuities. They offer tax advantages for philanthropic individuals and are generally best suited for people aged 70 or more. Your client can purchase an annuity directly through their charity. Usually a certain percentage or set amount of their funds goes to the charity right away as a donation, and they can use the tax credits from their charitable tax receipt in the current taxation year, or in any year in the next five years. The rest is invested in an annuity, and their annuity payments are either channeled to them through the charity, or from the insurance company.

Guaranteed Investment Accounts (GIAs)

These are the insurance industry's equivalent to GICs in the banking and credit union world. Advantages unique to GIAs include:

- Typically higher interest rates
- Flexibility of investments
- Daily interest investments

- Guaranteed interest rate investments with or without redeemable features
- Various terms, typically up to 10 years, and the ability to choose an end date
- Ability to lock in interest rates up to 45 days before deposit
- Potential creditor protection
- Security and safety – backed by the financial strength of Canada's insurance companies, and through Assuris, which also provides protection on amounts over the $100K insurance limit from the Canada Deposit Insurance Corporation coverage that is offered through Canadian banks and credit unions.

Segregated Funds

These are the mutual funds of the insurance world. These investments come with principal guarantees that offer significant estate and tax avoidance properties. As with other insurance products, clients can assign a charity to be a beneficiary of any residual funds remaining upon their death. Advantages unique to segregated funds are:

- *Insurance overlay of principal guarantees* – Depending on the contract, 75 - 100% of the principal invested is guaranteed if invested for a set period of time, usually 10 or 15 years. Some segregated funds allow for a reset of the principal guarantees when the market value rises. Resets normally push the maturity date ahead, usually 10 or 15 years from the reset date.

- *Death benefit guarantees* – Depending on the contract, beneficiaries can receive 100% of the principal or the market value, whichever is higher at the time of death. This guarantee removes the market risk from estate planning, which is increasing important as clients age, and don't have the time to recover from market downturns. Astute clients tend to insure their homes, so it makes sense that they also insure their investments, especially if they want to ensure their beneficiaries get the most income possible from these funds.

Potential creditor protection can be an important feature in many circumstances, and a risk reduction solution for many business owners.

Disadvantages of segregated funds:

- To get the maturity guarantee, money may need to be held until the date of maturity.
- Fees include the cost of insurance, so may be higher than most mutual funds. However, the advantages can make it well worth paying additional fees.

It's important to keep in mind that insurance company investments are best used to offer safety for savings in retirement planning, estate planning, financial planning and charitable gift planning needs. However, if your clients' needs and circumstances don't suit employing insurance company financial products, different options should be sought.

Chapter 7

TEN BENEFITS
OF USING INSURANCE FOR CHARITABLE GIVING

"One generation plants the tree…
another receives the shade."

— Chinese proverb

When considering the use of insurance for charitable giving, we must keep in mind all the various insurance products described in *Chapter 6*, including:

- life insurance
- annuities
- variable annuities
- segregated funds (the mutual funds of the insurance world)
- cash accounts
- insured Guaranteed Investment Accounts

Any or all of these can be effective pieces of a puzzle to provide solutions including income tax reduction, wealth replacement strategies, supporting family, and magnifying the positive effect of charitable giving.

Key benefits to employing insurance in charitable giving and estate planning that aren't available with other investments.

1. **Tax-free and direct:** Death benefits and residual income in life insurance and all other life insurance product benefits flow quickly and directly to their assigned beneficiaries and are not reduced by taxes. Being tax-free makes insurance a very effective financial tool in countless scenarios. To take advantage of the tax-free nature of insurance benefits, your client must *name a beneficiary rather than direct the proceeds to their estate*, where funds are subject to probate-related fees and taxes.

2. **Outside the estate:** Beneficiaries receive insurance-related funds outside the annuitant's estate. If you anticipate that your clients have the potential for conflict in the distribution of their estate according to their wishes laid out in their Will (or if they make the ill-advised choice not to have a Will), you can help your clients transfer their donation and other bequests to loved ones through insurance

products, which in most cases guarantees the beneficiary to receive the funds easily and directly.

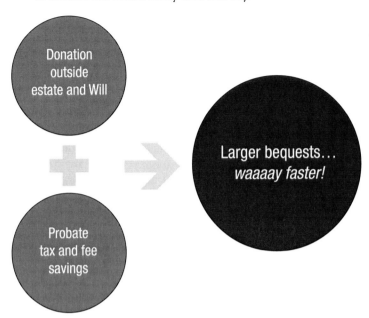

3. **Fast:** Once the insurance company receives the insurance claim, beneficiaries normally receive the proceeds within two to three weeks. When having a charity as a beneficiary, this is much more advantageous than charities waiting for gifts made through a Will, which can be decreased by probate-related fees and taxes if the gift is stated as a percentage, share or residue of the estate. Estate settlements can be delayed for years, until all aspects of the estate are dealt with.

4. **It lets more people be more generous than they've imagined:** The value of many life insurance and other insurance products grows in size over the insured person's lifetime, allowing people to donate insurance products that could be worth much more than the amount they initially invested in them, or the combined total of their premiums.

A small upfront investment can become a huge tax-free benefit. This makes insurance gifts very attractive to the thrifty. It also can significantly improve the positive impact anyone can have on their designated charities and the missions they support.

5. **Incontestability:** Beneficiary designations can't be changed by relatives or powers of attorney, who might otherwise challenge bequests. So normally these bequests won't get caught up in court battles, with the exception of possible challenges by dependent spouses and children. When assigning a charity to be a beneficiary, it is critical that the donor lists the charity's full legal name. With so many charities having similar names, there must be no doubt which charitable organization is the rightful beneficiary. Otherwise such gifts may be challenged. Adding the charitable registration number is a way to bulletproof the process.

6. **Privacy:** Only your client donor needs to know of the funds that will pass through insurance products to their beneficiaries. Nevertheless, it is highly advisable for your clients to leave their executor written instructions with other important papers such as their Will about the insurance policies and products they will find in the estate. Beneficiaries will only benefit if an insurance company is notified of an insured person's death.

7. **Creditor protection:** Insurance bequests with possible creditor protection are unlike bequests made through the Will that assign a residual amount to beneficiaries, therefore eliminating creditors jumping to the front of the line to reduce charitable gifts.

8. **Changing beneficiaries is simple:** By filling out a simple form, the owner of insurance products can change beneficiary designations. This is very important be-

cause it allows people to maintain control over the destination of their gifts. It is not unusual for donor priorities to change over their lifetime, or that they change their mind about which organization will receive a donation if the initial beneficiary does something that the donor disapproves of. Insurance donations provide flexibility. The only exception is if a person purchases a life insurance policy for the express purpose of making a charitable gift, and assigns the ownership of the policy to their charity of choice. Giving away the ownership is irrevocable (but does have its benefits – see *Chapter 8*).

9. **Annuities provide guaranteed income:** When used with life insurance in a giving scenario often referred to as the "back-to-back strategy," annuity payments can be directed to paying the premiums on life insurance policies used to generate a charitable donation. This becomes very important because it is not unusual for gifted life insurance policies to fail – donors change their mind about making a gift to a certain charity and stop making premium payments, or they become financially or mentally incapable of continuing to make payments on gifted policies. Annuities are ideal to guarantee that gifted policies will stay in force and will fulfill the philanthropic dreams of your clients.

Annuities can also allow people to be more generous in their lifetime by supplying your clients with guaranteed income for life, which could free up cash to give during their lifetime, when they can appreciate seeing the results of their giving in action.

10. **Amount of your client's charitable bequest will be guaranteed** when giving a gift of life insurance or insurance products.

For example, if your client owns a segregated fund (an

insurance company's "mutual fund") into which she has invested $50,000. She assigns her charity to be the fund's beneficiary, so it will receive any residual amount left in the fund when she dies. Even though a charity is designed as beneficiary, your client has the benefit of retaining control over that investment during her lifetime, should unexpected expenses later arise or beneficiaries need to be changed.

In the end, let's assume your client never had to touch the fund and her charity remained its beneficiary. However, the stock market crashed before she died, making her fund worth $35,000 upon her passing. Because of insurance company 100% principal guarantee, her charity still gets the original $50,000. If the market was in an upswing upon the time of her death, making the fund worth more than $50,000, then her charity would have received the higher market value. Furthermore, assets without guarantees may subject to further losses while an estate gets settled.

After the insurance company is officially informed of your client's death, it will send the charity the final value of her fund within two to three weeks. The charity will then issue the estate a charitable tax receipt, which can be used to further reduce estate taxes, or if the tax credits exceed this amount, the balance can be used to recover taxes paid in the year prior to your client's death. In the end, your client's other beneficiaries will receive more, due to these tax credits.

Alternately, here's what would happen if your client wanted to leave the residue of her $50,000 in non-registered investments to a charity. First, because beneficiaries cannot be assigned to these accounts, your client would have to note in her Will her intentions to have her charity receive the residue of her mutual fund.

When she passes away, her investments will go through probate, delaying the gift and reducing its value by the probate-related fees and taxes. It will be further reduced by estate taxes. In the end, her charity would likely receive about $45,000 after about one year, once her estate is officially cleared through the probate process and the assets are distributed by the executor. The charitable tax receipt issued will be proportionately smaller, also reducing the amount going to her other beneficiaries.

Chapter 8

BRINGING IT HOME
FOR YOUR CLIENTS

"As I started getting rich, I started thinking,
'What the hell am I doing with all this money?'
You have to learn to give."

— Ted Turner, American media mogul
and philanthropist

Help your clients give more, in life and after death, by integreting insurance products in estate planning

A friend once told me that he couldn't be "logicked" into buying something, or doing something he doesn't want to do.

Most of us behave in this same way. How we view money, how we spend and save and our level of desire for self-sufficiency all influence how we react to events and take subsequent action.

Of course, our behaviours change over time, with the evolution of our vision of the future and what we value the most. And with age come decisions on what we want to leave to loved ones, and how we can use philanthropy to leave a lasting and meaningful legacy.

When we drill down to what's most important to us — including charitable giving — we can use resources of time, effort, skills and money to specifically meet those passions and goals.

When it comes to financial management, you can help clients see past the obvious solutions by integrating tools that allow people to do more with what they have.

After you've learned your clients' goals, it's important to know if they have a legal Will. This is the one document that most people choose to define what happens to their assets and contemplate how they can leave a lasting legacy after they're gone.

A Will is an important and necessary part of financial and estate planning, but it can become a hindrance if not reviewed periodically, to ensure its directions remain relevant as time passes. In reality, most people draft their Will and then keep it in a safe place for their executor to employ decades later. They think that changing a Will isn't worth the hassle or the cost.

By understanding how your clients' Will is structured, you can sometimes reveal changes in the way their finances are organized (in death and in life alike) to allow them to do more with what they have.

In this realm, insurance and insurance products can offer flexibility that clients can't get with a Will. Insurance products can give clients the cost- and hassle-free ability to quickly and easily change beneficiaries if priorities change, and create assurances that their funds will go exactly where they should, in the most timely and cost-efficient manner possible.

Client Goal: Leave more to family and charity.

Insurance Solution: Transferring GICs, mutual funds, cash, registered savings and other invested funds into similar insurance products.

You can help your clients take advantage of insurance products' ability to assign a beneficiary and allow funds to flow quickly and simply to heirs and charities outside their estate by transferring investments held in banks and credit unions into similar products offered by insurance companies. Although income taxes will still have to be paid on these products, the funds are not considered part of the estate, so they don't go through probate nor will they be reduced by probate taxes or fees.

For example, a parent has told you that he intends to leave the residue of his mutual funds to his son. He can sell these funds and use the money to buy insurance company segregated funds with similar attributes, then assign his son as beneficiary.

Client Fear: Client hangs on to appreciated assets to avoid capital gains tax.

Insurance Solution: Use life insurance as a wealth replacement tool, or as a charitable gift.

Out of an aversion for paying capital gains tax, it's amazing how many people hang on to appreciated assets — stocks, real estate, or collectibles like classic cars or works of art — even if they have no need for them.

Of course they may have a legitimate concerns. If someone starts selling off assets during their lifetime, they may run into financial issues such as getting bumped into a higher tax bracket. Worse yet, their income-tested government pensions like Old Age Security might get reduced or eliminated entirely when their income exceeds certain levels.

If these assets remain in their estate when they die, capital gains tax can dramatically decrease the inheritance they wish to go to family and charities. Family members often have no choice but to sell these assets to pay the taxes owing.

Your client can solve this problem by buying life insurance to offset anticipated estate taxes.

If they are philanthropically minded, they can also use the insurance policy as a **charitable gift**. By assigning a charity to be a beneficiary of an insurance policy (whether it is a new policy or an existing policy that no longer is needed for the original purpose under which it was bought), the person will get estate get tax relief through to the charitable tax receipt issued to the estate for death benefit received by the charity.

I should note that it is possible for a charity to be named as the co-beneficiary of a split-value life insurance policy, with the charity receiving a percentage of the final death benefit, split with one or more other beneficiaries.

An added benefit in making a charitable gift in this way is that clients have the option of increasing or decreasing the percentage the charity will receive should family or emergency needs arise, or assigning a different charity if their giving priorities change.

If the charity is the beneficiary of the policy at the time of the donor's death, the death benefit gets transferred to the charity within two to three weeks after the executor sends in the claim to the insurance company. The charity then issues the tax receipt to the donor's estate.

Charitable tax credits can be used against 100% of the donor's net income in the year of his or her death, and if they exceed the taxes owing, can also be used against 100% of the donor's net income in the year before his or her death.

Client goal: Client wants to make a legacy donation that has significant impact, and would also like tax relief during her lifetime.
or
Client fear: Client wants to leave a significant gift to charity in her Will and would like to avoid the possibility of any challenges to her bequest.

Insurance solution: Assigning a charity to be the *owner and beneficiary* of a new or unneeded insurance policy

For the purpose of making a dedicated legacy gift that is incontestable,* your client can guarantee that her registered charity receives her donation by buying a life insurance policy (or donating a policy that was purchased for a reason that no longer exists) and assigning a charity as *owner and beneficiary* of the policy. Your client then pays all the premiums on a policy.

Because the registered charity was made the owner of her policy, it considers all of her premium payments on the policy as tax-receiptable charitable gifts. Charities usually send tax receipts to such donors once a year, reflecting the combined total of all premiums paid over a calendar year. Charities learn the exact amount of premiums paid the previous calendar year from the insurance company each January.

* If your client's children, or her spouse, are considered to be legal dependents, they might contest such an insurance donation. Otherwise, the donation is guaranteed on policies that are in force when the donor dies.

I bring up the issue of charitable gifts being contested for the simple reason that money can make regular people do things that are dramatically out of character.

I've spoken with several fundraisers who have shared stories of adult children legally contesting charitable bequests because the child believes the money is theirs. In fact, some fundraisers have lost bequests that donors had revealed they planned to give to their organization, or have seen them significantly decrease in size, because in the donor's dying days, his or her kids — with a lawyer in tow — convince their weakened parent that the charitable gift in his or her Will is abnormally high and that an "appropriate" gift is much lower. Standing at the bedside, a pre-drafted revised Will is pulled out and signed off, and the kids walk away with more from the estate!

Much of this can be avoided when your clients involve their whole family in a conversation about their charitable legacy. Often the way to bulletproof their charitable gifts and legacies to all their beneficiaries is to effectively remove it from their estate by using gifts of insurance.

Client goal: Your client wants to leave a large gift using insurance, and the most cost-effective life insurance policy is a life pay.

The challenge: Charities often see gifts of life-pay insurance policies fail when donors stop paying premiums.

Insurance solution: Employing short-pay life insurance or whole life insurance backed up by a dedicated annuity – the "Back-to-Back Strategy" or an "Insured Annuity" increases the chance that gifted life insurance policies achieve the donor's intended effect.

A lot of fundraisers are reluctant to promote giving through insurance for a few reasons.

First, they prefer to promote gifts made through the Will, which they refer to as bequests. They are easy to explain and for donors to understand. For some charities, bequests represent a large source of regular income that they don't want to put in jeopardy.

Secondly, insurance can be complicated, and some fundraisers don't feel they understand it well enough to effectively explain its use to their donors, nor can they answer detailed questions donors may have for them. Our companion volume, ***Multiplying Generosity: Creatively using insurance to increase legacy gifts***, dedicated to educating fundraisers, should help solve this problem.

Finally, some fundraisers may dislike gifts of life insurance because many gifted life-pay insurance policies fail when donors stop paying the premiums. This may be partly due to the fact that some charities over-simplify their promotion of gifts of insurance, saying: "You can donate insurance policies you no longer need."

This can lead to people dumping T-100 policies on charities, expecting that charities will continue paying the premiums to receive a big final gift. Yet most organizations can't afford to do so. In some circumstances, a charity may find other regular donors to pick up the premium payments, but usually, if a policy fails a charity will simply cash out the policy, which can result in a large potential donation being left on the table.

There are different reasons why donors stop paying premiums on gifted policies. Some of these include:

- They no longer can afford the premiums.

- The donor's mental capacities slip, and so does their capacity to efficiently take care of their finances. Their power of attorney steps in to help with financial management, and isn't aware of the insurance policy and therefore doesn't continue payments.

- The charity has done something that annoyed the donor.

- Most people don't give monthly gifts to the same charity, year after year, for decades, until they die. As people grow older and their interests and priorities change, they shift their charitable giving to other causes that are now closer to their heart. They see their premiums on gifted policies as donations, and when their giving priorities change, they can stop paying their premiums.

Short-pay policies

Policies that can be entirely paid off in five to ten years can help donors achieve a goal, and then when their policy is paid off, they can easily start a new policy and move on to another charitable goal. This option can be attractive for younger people in the prime earning years; people who want to give back to a cause that's affected them; those who want to support several causes; and those who like leveraging the power of insurance but don't want to pay for life. Short-pay policies usually have higher premiums, but are still an affordable option for the person who wishes to make a gift that in the end is much larger than the sum of their premiums. This story illustrates the benefits of donating short-pay policies.

Mary is a healthy 50-year-old Ontarian, and a respected director in her company. She wants to use the multiplying power of life insurance to make a substantial gift to one of her favourite charities.

Mary buys a $50,000 permanent life insurance policy, chosen specifically because it can be paid up in any time frame she wishes. Since Mary is in her peak earning years, she decides to pay up the entire policy in five years. She names a favourite charity as the policy's owner and beneficiary. She then arranges a meeting with this charity, and instructs them to direct her policy's death benefit to the area of their work that touches her most.

Her monthly premiums are $350 a month (or $4,200 a year). Mary is delighted that the charitable tax receipts she gets for her premiums gives her a tax credit of about 41%** of their value from her annual income taxes.

Over five years, Mary pays $21,000 in premiums, but thanks to the tax credits they generate, her real cost to purchase the $50,000 policy benefiting her charity is only $12,600.

After her policy is paid up, Mary is so thrilled by her ability to make a significant continuing impact on this charity's work that she purchases another policy benefiting another favourite charity!

*Note: The amount of the premium reflected in this example will not reflect everyone's personal circumstances. The value of premiums a person pays are based on his or her age, health, weight, occupation, the type and value of insurance policy chosen, and the time frame in which he or she wishes to pay its premiums.

**Canadian charitable tax credits vary from about 40 to 50%, depending on the province or territory a donor lives in. In

Ontario, the tax credit is approximately 41%.

Insured Annuities, a.k.a. The Back-to-Back Strategy

This option can work in many circumstances, including the story of Frank in *Chapter 1*. Here is another example that allows a 65-year-old mother to accomplish many life goals by bringing insurance and annuities into her greater financial plan.

Eva is a retired 65-year-old Canadian widow and mother of two living in a rental apartment in Calgary, Alberta. Eva has three key goals in life:

- To live comfortably.
- To leave her children residual funds from her estate.
- To donate generously to her favourite charity.

Eva is living off Old Age Security and Canada Pension Plan funds, deductions from RRIF savings currently worth $150,000, and $1,836 per year in after-tax income made on 2.7% interest earned on $100,000 in non-registered GICs. With an income of less than $39,000 a year, Eva's tax rate is 22%.

Eva has assigned her charity as the beneficiary of the residue of her RRIF, and has bequeathed whatever is left of her GIC savings to her children.

But Eva's interest income is low and the cost of living in Calgary is going up. Eva feels she is eating too quickly into her RRIF to pay her bills, and worries she can't achieve any of her goals if she outlives her money.

She goes to her financial advisor to ask him if there is a better way for her to manage her finances and to improve her income without increasing her investment risk. He guides her through some highly beneficial strategic changes.

- Eva purchases a $100,000 whole life insurance policy that will grow in value over time and assigns her children as its co-beneficiaries. Her annual premiums are $2,815.

- Using her $100,000 in GICs, Eva purchases an annuity. Her insurance broker ensures she gets the highest rate of return at that time. Although Eva no longer retains access to this capital, her annuity guarantees her after-tax income of $5,707 annually, for life.

- Eva uses $2,694 from her annual payments to cover her insurance premiums. She's thrilled this will guarantee her children an inheritance of a minimum of $50,000 each. She also bequeaths any tax refunds generated by her charitable tax credits to her children.

- To help Eva live more comfortably, she now has $2,897 in after-tax dollars from her annuity payment. Because of this increased income, Eva reduces her RRIF payments, further reducing her income tax.

Eva peacefully passes away, 20 years later, at age 85.

This chart allows you to see how Eva's Back-to-Back Strategy has allowed her to achieve her life's goals.

Eva's original financial plan	Eva's new back-to-back strategy
Eva's annual income	**Eva's annual income**
From $100,000 GIC earning 2.7% **$2,700**	From $100,000 Annuity **$5,707**
Income tax payable at 22% ($594)	Life Insurance premium ($2,694)
	Income tax paid on Income tax paid on taxable amount of annuity payment @22% ($115.61)
Eva's net GIC income $2,106	**Eva's net Annuity income $2897.39**
Eva's estate	**Eva's estate**
Charitable legacy gift	**Charitable legacy gift**
Donation of RRIF **$80,000**	Donation of RRIF **$100,000**
Charitable tax credits **$40,000**	Charitable tax credits **$50,000**
Eva's estate taxes	**Eva's estate taxes**
Income tax on RRIF ($25,600)	Income tax on RRIF ($28,650)
Minus tax credits from donation ($40,000)	Minus tax credits from donation ($50,000)
Income tax owed $0	Income tax owed $0
Probate taxes and related fees **($5,000)**	Probate taxes and related fees **$0**
Tax credit balance of $14,400 generates a refund of $5,760 from previous year's taxes	**Tax credit balance of $21,350 generates a refund of $8,580 from previous year's taxes**
Eva's bequest to her children	**Eva's bequest to her children**
GIC residue $100,000	Life insurance policy (value after 20 yrs.) $130,000 (tax free)
Minus probate-related fees ($5,000), plus $5,760 tax refund from previous year (due to charitable tax credits)	Plus $8,580 tax refund from previous year (due to charitable tax credits)
Total bequest to children $100,760	**Total bequest to children $138,580**

There are three significant advantages helping Eva fulfill her legacy goals that result from the same money simply being rearranged with the help of Eva's financial advisor: higher annual income, significantly more money to charity as a beneficiary, and more money to the kids as beneficiaries!

Note: In this example, Eva's annuity income was determined based on the best rates available in December 2014, and a prediction of Eva's lifespan using mortality tables. As an Alberta resident, Eva's charitable tax credit is almost 50%; tax credits vary from province to province. This example shows how it is possible that a large charitable tax receipt could significantly reduce or eliminate taxes owing on the estate, but depending on the value of the donation and estate, this may not be the case for every individual. However, if charitable tax credits are greater than all taxes owed in a donor's terminal year, the unused balance can be applied to recover taxes paid in the year prior to the donor's passing – which provides another opportunity to pass on more to loved ones and charities.

Client donation opportunity: Parents purchased a policy for a purpose that no longer exists – e.g. to provide for a child if the parents pass away unexpectedly, but the child is now an adult.

Insurance solution: Donate a fully-funded, unneeded life insurance policy to a good cause.

This is the most common way donors use life insurance as a donation. For the policy to be of value to a charity, the donor would have made sufficient premium payments to date to have accumulated a sufficient cash value within the policy to pay all future premiums and keep the policy active until the death of the insured person. An in-force illustration will indicate if the policy is guaranteed never to lapse.

This fictional example illustrates how such a gift can be put to good use by a favourite charity.

Ghislaine Forest, President of the Delectable Edibles Bakeries empire, decides to name The Kids Can Bake Foundation as the beneficiary of a fully-funded, self-sustaining $500,000 life insurance policy she no longer needs. In case Ghislaine experiences a future family emergency, she wants the option of changing the beneficiary of her policy to a family member, so she assigns the Foundation as her policy's beneficiary, and retains the ownership of the policy.

In anticipation that the Foundation will receive the policy's death benefit, Ghislaine spoke with Foundation staff and arranged for the Foundation to endow the proceeds of her policy. Its annual interest will fund scholarships for promising bakers, given in the name of Ghislaine's late mother, Jeanne Sicotte, the founder of Delectable Edibles.

Ghislaine did not get charitable tax receipts for the premiums she continued to pay on her policy until her death. But when the Foundation became the beneficiary of her policy, the $500,000 charitable tax receipt sent to Ghislaine's estate generated a huge tax credit that allowed Ghislaine to leave an additional $250,000 to family members.

Client goal: Having enough money to live on until they die, and leaving a gift to charity, if possible.

Insurance Solution: Annuities, or Charitable Gift Annuities offered directly to donors by charities.

Annuities

For clients who are anxious about outliving their funds, especially during times of low interest rates, annuities offered by insurance companies are an increasingly popular solution. You can remind your clients that they have the option of assigning their favourite charity to be the beneficiary of any residue remaining in their annuity when they pass away.

You may also have retired clients who own annuities that they don't need for retirement income. If these clients are insurable, they can supersize the value of their annuity funds by using this income to fund the premiums on an insurance policy, which can allow them to leave more to their charities and/or their kids.

These clients can purchase a life insurance policy, and start using annuity income to pay for its premiums. Yes, the interest on the new income from the annuity will be taxable, but the significantly greater death benefit from the life insurance would be tax-free for beneficiaries. And of course any charitable donation resulting from including a charitable beneficiary can help reduce estate taxes, allowing your client to leave even more to other beneficiaries.

Help your clients with greater charitable goals

Charitable Gift Annuities

Some of your clients may learn that their favourite charity offers Charitable Gift Annuities, which may also be known as Gift Plus Annuities. This kind of annuity is most often offered by larger organizations that have long-term mandates.

In a contractual agreement, a person (or a couple) gives the charity at least $100,000 in cash or securities, or as much as the donor wishes. The minimum amount may vary from charity to the charity.

Usually a minimum of 20 per cent is retained by the charity as an immediate donation, and the charity issues a tax receipt to the donor for that amount. The charity uses the balance of the funds to purchase a prescribed annuity through a broker or directly from a favoured insurance company. The charity becomes the owner and beneficiary of the annuity, and all annuity payments are set up to go to the donor.

As with regular annuities, the donor pays tax only on the interest portion of their payment. Payments to older donors may be entirely tax-free, giving them a return that could be up to 50% greater than they could realize with other types of investments or interest generated by savings.

Sample charitable gift annuity of $100,000 with $20,000 (20%) deducted as an immediate charitable donation

	Monthly Income[1]	Annual Income[1]	Annual Taxable Income	Gift & Receipt[2]	Annual Rate of Return[3]
Female, 77	$565.37	$6,784.44	$0	$20,000	6.78%
Male, 72	$544.54	$6,534.48	$0	$20,000	6.53%

[1] Annuity income is guaranteed for the rest of the annuitant's life, even if all capital invested has already been returned to annuitant.

[2] Value of charitable tax credit is between 40-50% of the gift, depending on where donor lives in Canada. Tax credits can be applied against present income taxes on up to 75% of annual income, or against income taxes for up to 5 years going forward.

[3] Annuity rates can change frequently. This rate is as of late December 2014.

Client goal: Avoid capital gains tax and be very generous.

Insurance solution: Marrying gifts of securities and insurance products to generate a large legacy gift.

Donations of appreciated securities have become a very popular giving option for Canadians since the law was amended to forgive the payment of all capital gains tax on charitable donations of appreciated securities. If your client's circumstances make it unlikely that she'll be able to avoid potential capital gains taxes and she is insurable, she can supersize her donation by purchasing a life insurance policy, assigning her charity as its owner and beneficiary, and making a gift of securities to that same charity. She then directs the charity to use the funds from the security to cover the cost of all of the premiums on the insurance policy.

This is a different example of how someone hindered by a capital gains tax aversion can rethink his finances and incorporate insurance products to live comfortably, be more generous to family, provide charity with timely gifts by donating securities, and fulfill his guilty pleasure to give less to the taxman.

. . . .

Ray Brown is a reasonably healthy "73-years-young!" widower who lives in Ontario (Canada). During the initial conversation with his financial advisor, Ray shared that he worked for 38 years for the phone company, put money into registered retirement savings, has savings in an investment account, and has a decent pension. After adding in Canada Pension Plan (CPP) and Old Age Security (OAS) income, Ray believes that he can easily cover his needs for the rest of his life.

Ray also noted that his son and daughter have solid careers and are both very well off. He's proud that they followed his example and tuck away money each year for their retirement, and their kids' university education.

Because Ray has involved his family in making decisions about charitable donations in the past, Ray told his kids that when he dies, he will make a bequest in both of their names to a local charity his family has long supported – a small community-based social service organization that supports homeless youth. He also let his kids know that he'd leave money to his three grandchildren, whom he loves spending time with.

In his Will, he designated the residue of his estate to be divided equally between his grandkids, minus a charitable bequest of $380,000 to his charity. Because Ray defined a fixed-amount donation in his Will, as he gets older, he's nervous about this choice because if he needs the money later to cover increasing healthcare costs, he'd feel guilty spending it. Ideally, he wants to maintain control of his funds, should he need them.

Ray let the Executive Director of this charity know that he hopes to leave a large gift to the organization in his Will. He was surprised to learn that this organization can benefit more if he can make his donation in annual smaller gifts than giving it all at once, after Ray passes away. Wanting to do right by the charity, Ray asks his advisor how he can to make some changes to the way he planned to support the organization, while remaining in control during his lifetime over a large amount of what he wants to give to his charity.

Ray keeps a $435,000 investment account in his back pocket, just in case he needs money sometime down the road. The account has grown over the years. He's very reluctant to make any changes to it because changes or withdrawals will trigger capital gains tax, and Ray detests paying more tax than he feels he should.

Ray's Registered Retired Income Fund (RRIF), now worth $320,000, was purchased through his bank. Ray has named his family members and his charity as beneficiaries (with the balance of the charity's donation coming from other estate assets).

Challenges to be overcome in Ray's plan

In analyzing the way Ray's legacy wishes are currently structured, his advisor considered these important issues:

1. He needs to find an efficient way for Ray to stagger the donations to his charity.

2. Over the years, one of the securities in Ray's investment account has grown dramatically, and it now represents more than 50% of the account's total value. With too many eggs in one basket, Ray's savings are at high risk. To make matters worse, Ray's desire to avoid paying capital gains tax is stopping him from making good financial decisions that can help him today and his estate tomorrow.

3. After Ray dies, the value of his registered plan will be added to his total income for that year, triggering taxes at the highest rate: a little over 50 percent. When his advisor told Ray that his estate would owe more than $160,000 in taxes on his registered income alone, he moaned, "I don't want the taxman to be my largest beneficiary. I'd prefer that more to go to my family and my charity."

4. If Ray makes a legacy gift from his RRIF and other savings, his bequest will be tied up in the probate process for about a year. Ray would prefer that his charity gets his donation faster.

Creating a better financial outcome by including insurance products

Ray's financial advisor suggested a strategy that he had used for many other clients – a no-cost approach that rearranges Ray's financial picture to lower taxes, and allow him to be more generous to his family and charities.

Step 1: Realize philanthropic goals and offset taxes

Ray can do better for himself and his charity by donating the $380,000, broken into smaller gifts, while he is alive.

Ray's advisor does the math and realizes that Ray can donate $40,000 each year to his charity. He suggests Ray makes his gift by donating appreciated securities held in his **non-registered** investment account, rather than securities he holds in his RRIF. He explained this offered great benefits:

a. The Canadian Revenue Agency waives the capital gains tax on donations of appreciated securities – but only when they are held in non-registered accounts.

b. The charitable tax receipts Ray receives for these donations will decrease his annual taxes.

c. Giving in this way won't affect Ray's income and taxes, compared to what would happen if Ray donated cash or securities withdrawn from his RRIF, possibly generating an unwanted a clawback or cancellation of Ray's Old Age Security benefits.

   Note: OAS benefits change regularly so check with Service Canada for exact figures based on individual circumstances. Source: http://bit.ly/1MlpDjw

Ray loved being able to both reduce his taxes and witness the impact of his giving during his lifetime. Win-win!

Ray was advised to directly transfer his securities to his charity, since capital gains exemptions don't apply if he sells his stocks and donates the cash.

Knowing that Ray was concerned that large annual gifts may place him in financial hardship if his health or other circumstances change, requiring additional funds to live on, his advisor came up with this creative solution.

Step 2: Ensuring Ray has enough to live comfortably for the rest of his life, while remaining in control of his money

To diversify Ray's savings and lower his risk, Ray was directed to annually withdraw from his RRIF the same amount he donated to charity. He was to take this money and buy guaranteed low-risk segregated funds through an insurance company (more on this in Step 3).

The charitable tax receipt Ray receives for his annual donations offset the taxes owing on his RRIF withdrawals. Ray is thrilled about that.

Because there is an immediate requirement of 30% with-holding tax by his bank on Ray's RRIF withdrawals, and a time lag until the funds can be recouped at tax time using charitable tax credits, Ray is advised to make his withdrawals late in the calendar year.

Step 3: Using insurance products to help fulfill all of Ray's goals

Ray designated his grandchildren as the beneficiaries of the segregated funds he purchased. Ray believes his grandkids can benefit more from receiving their inheritance in stages, so he chooses the annuity settlement option, offered by most insurance companies on many of their products. This meters out their inheritance over time rather than giving them a lump sum when he passes away.

Ray then went to his lawyer and amended his Will to reflect his new estate plan.

Benefits Ray received by making these financial changes:

- Ray gained control over how his beneficiaries receive their inheritance.

- By making his beneficiaries the recipients of segregated funds, their inheritance/donation does not go through probate, is not diminished by taxes, and will start flowing to them within two to three weeks of Ray's executor sending the insurance company Ray's death certificate and claim form.

- Charitable gifts made during Ray's lifetime eliminated taxes payable on his annual registered account withdrawals.

- Giving to his charity during his lifetime allowed Ray to wit-ness the results of his donations.

- Ray takes great delight in giving to help homeless kids in his community, instead of giving to the taxman.

- RRIF funds were used to reduce the level of investment risk in his investment account.
- Ray maintains control over his investment dollars for life, just in case.
- Ray significantly reduced the tax load on his estate, leaving more for all of his beneficiaries.

Client goal: To guarantee that their charity receives a donation of a specific size.

Insurance Solution: Gifts of Segregated Funds.

Segregated funds are the mutual funds of the insurance world. They present a guaranteed donation opportunity because they offer investment growth and guarantee that their value will never drop below the principal amount invested in it, even if the value of the products held within the fund drops. Advise your client to also invest in a segregated fund that can increase in value in bull markets. Remind them that the charitable tax receipt generated by the gift can help to offset the estate taxes owing on the fund.

In contrast, if the market value of a mutual fund donated through a Will is depressed at the time of the donor's death, the charity's gift will be smaller than intended. The gift will also be decreased by probate-related fees and taxes, and estate taxes owed on the fund, which result in both a smaller donation and lower charitable tax credits for the estate.

Client goal: To bequeath a GIC to charity through the Will.

Insurance Solution: Create a larger, virtually incontestable gift by transferring the GIC funds into an insured GIC.

If your client already has a bequest set aside in a Guaranteed Investment Certificate (GIC) in a bank, he or she can offer their charity a faster and somewhat larger gift by simply transferring the funds in the GIC (upon maturity) into an insurance company GIC. Not only do insurance company GICs typically offer higher interest rates, your clients can specifically assign the beneficiary of these insured GICs to their favourite charity, making the donation virtually incontestable (except by a dependent spouse or dependent children). Although your client's estate will still owe income taxes on interest earned in the GIC, the taxes will be offset by the charitable tax receipt issued to the estate.

This simple switch takes the donation out of your client's Will and estate. Therefore it won't be reduced by probate taxes, nor lawyers' and executors' fees. It will also go directly to their charity within two to three weeks of the insurance company receiving the claim.

Client goal: Would like to leave a legacy donation to charity, but needs to take care of family first.

Insurance Solution: Assigning a charity to be a contingent beneficiary to a life insurance policy or any insurance product.

Those who need their insurance policies or residue of any other insurance products to provide financial security for their family members can still possibly be philanthropic by naming a charity as a contingent beneficiary, which allows the charity to receive the death benefit should those named as beneficiaries be no longer alive when the insured person dies.

Building on the Charity Child concept mentioned in *Chapter 4*, it is possible for a client to be able to divide the proceeds from an insurance policy or possible residue from insurance products to more than one beneficiary. For example, a parent could name both their child and a charity to be co-beneficiaries of one policy. The policy owner can also assign what percentage each beneficiary receives.

Client goal: Wants to leave a generous legacy gift to charity, but isn't sure yet what he wants the money to accomplish, nor which charity should get it.

Insurance Solution: Donate a life insurance policy to a donor advised fund or community foundation.

You will run into clients who want to be philanthropic, but haven't made up their mind yet about which charities they wish to support, or how much they'll receive. Others may have a pool of assets, cash or an insurance policy that they want to split between several organizations.

A solution may be for your client to either set up a Donor Advised Fund or a private foundation.

Donor Advised Funds (DAFs)

Donor Advised Funds can be established at most banks, Community Foundations (see great advisor resources at the Community Foundations of Canada website www.cfc-fcc.ca), or directly through some charitable foundations. DAFs set minimum amounts they will assist to manage – from $10,000 to amounts in the hundreds of thousands. A client may have to shop around to find the best fit.

Setting up a DAF is much easier than administering a private foundation.

Says Malcolm Burrows, Head of Philanthropic Advisory Services for Scotiabank's Donor Advised Fund, Aqueduct Foundation, "DAFs can be funded by contributions made throughout the client's lifetime, and/or can include estate cash and assets [like insurance policy benefits] freed up after the client dies. Their DAF becomes the owner and beneficiary of the funds, and as registered charities, will issue charitable tax receipts to the contributors for those funds. Fund managers then follow the directions of the client and become the facilitating bridge to dispense the funds according to the client's wishes."

Donors choose which organizations will receive donations, and how often or when these gifts are made. Many parents like to involve their children and grandchildren in these decisions to pass on the philanthropic torch.

DAFs can facilitate anonymous gifts to charities. However, DAF Fund Managers like to encourage donors to establish a relationship with their charities. This allows donors to learn more about the organization's needs and goals, which can help them direct their donations in ways that have the biggest impact on the aspect of the organization's work that interests them most.

Although there are no start-up costs to set up a Donor Advised Fund, there are annual fees to cover administration costs such as distributing donations. Fees vary, with the lowest being 0.5%. Individuals who have never used the services of a lawyer or accountant may find it expensive.

Private Foundations

In case your client is interested in possibly creating a private foundation for the purpose of charitable giving, there are many legalities to follow since foundations must be accepted by the Canada Revenue Agency as a registered charity. They are controlled by an individual or family through a board made up of a majority of directors at non-arm's length. It is not allowed to engage in any for-profit business activity. As a registered charity, there is governmental monitoring, including producing annual audited statements.

There may also be ongoing fund management fees. A rule of thumb is that to be cost effective, generally a client should be able to dedicate a minimum of $1 million. These funds can include the proceeds of insurance policies.

Private foundations do allow people to annuitize their giving or give over time, and have complete control over allocation of funds.

Private foundations are legally obliged to make owner's information publicly available. This can either be a problem if clients want to make anonymous donations, or a benefit to those who wish to let the world know of their philanthropy.

For more information, refer to the Philanthropic Foundations Canada's website: www.pfc.ca.

Client goal: Estate management made easy: Simplify distribution of estate assets and reduce assets going through probate.

Insurance Solution: Distribute estate assets through life insurance or insurance products.

Proceeds normally flow directly to the beneficiaries of any insurance products within a few weeks of the insurance company receiving the claim. Depending on the product, estate taxes may be owed on the funds being distributed.

Any funds distributed through life insurance and all insurance products such as annuities, GICs, money market funds and segregated funds (the mutual funds of the insurance world) occur outside of the estate and therefore bypass probate (known as a Certificate of Appointment of Estate Trustee and the Estate Administration Tax in Ontario, Canada).

Avoiding probate can be a huge advantage when a client's family or estate trustee is depending on these funds to cover their own expenses or funeral costs, cover charitable bequests, pay taxes, or cover outstanding bills or other debt. If assets must go through probate, there is extensive paperwork, and all funds are frozen for the duration of the process, which is more often than not up to a year or longer.

Access to assets undergoing probate to pay for necessities such as ongoing bills like utility charges is usually permission-based. The executor needs to go to the financial institution (with the death certificate, a notarized copy of the Will, and the bills to be paid in hand) and the institution will in turn pay the bills from the estate account on the estate's behalf. Most institutions also charge the estate additional fees for this service.

There are also fees associated with the probate process that include lawyers' fees and accountant fees.

The probate taxes (known in Ontario as the Estate Administration Tax) differs according to where your clients live, and is a percentage of the market value of the estate's assets.

Although these fees and taxes may not amount to much, avoiding these costs and inconvenience to the estate is often a strong incentive for many people to look at alternatives.

Client goal: Generate the largest possible charitable gift by donating insured registered savings.

Insurance Solution: Transfer registered savings into insurance company registered products.

You can help your clients give more to charity, pay less tax and generate a larger inheritance for beneficiaries by making use of registered insurance products.

When a charity is designated as the beneficiary of a RRSP/RRIF held with an insurance company, the gift is deemed to have been made immediately before the donor's death, provided that the RRSP/RRIF assets are transferred to the charity within 36 months of his or her death. Since the funds remaining in an RRSP/RRIF are treated as income in the year of death, the charitable credit should eliminate most if not all of the income tax on these funds.

Making a gift of funds registered through an insurance company offers an additional bonus: the donation (and resulting charitable tax credits) can often be 6% to 10% more than the total pre-tax value due to the elimination of probate taxes and estate administration fees by the executor, lawyer and accountant.

So helping your client make it easier and less costly to administer the final estate will certainly gain you additional loyalty.

Client goal: Transfer major assets to the kids after death, and support the good works of charities.

Insurance Solution: Using a gift of life insurance to cover the capital gains tax upon the transfer of the cottage to the younger generation.

Often the best way to transfer certain assets to a younger generation — including homes, cottages and expensive personal items — is to designate them to beneficiaries through the Will.

Assets including second homes, vacation properties and

investment accounts, are deemed sold upon death, and the estate or the beneficiaries have to cover the capital gains taxes, which can be significant. Often beneficiaries need to sell these properties to pay the taxes owing. Life insurance can be used to replace the taxes owing, or even to fulfill their philanthropic goals to cover the tax hit, as seen in this example.

. . . .

Sarah, who's turning 65 in one year, expects to keep her cottage for the rest of her life, then leave it to her two kids. Her financial advisor pointed out that upon her death, the cottage transfer will occur, but that her cottage will be deemed sold, and her kids or her estate will bear the brunt of a large capital gains tax bill. Based on today's value, the tax bill would be about $75,000. Sarah worries that her kids may be forced to sell their beloved cottage to pay the capital gains tax.

Sarah's advisor knows that Sarah makes generous annual gifts to her charities, and begins to explore how tax credits generated by charitable donations can both save the family cottage, and help out Sarah's favourite charities – smaller local organizations that she sees having a direct impact on people in her community.

The advisor first suggested that Sarah could have the biggest impact on her charities by purchasing a $150,000 life insurance policy that could grow over her lifetime, and by naming her favourite charities as equal beneficiaries of the death benefit. He pointed out that on her death, the donation of the policy would generate charitable tax credits that could wipe out the taxes due on the cottage.

Sarah expressed a concern that local charities like those she prefers can come and go, depending on evolving needs in her community. She was concerned that charities assigned as beneficiaries may not be around when she passes.

Her advisor remembered speaking to the CEO of a Community Foundation at a Mind*path*™ seminar he had attended in Toronto (www.mindpath.ca). The CEO explained how the Foundation helps facilitate donor gifts, and that the Foundation itself was a registered charity. So, the advisor suggested that Sarah makes her local Community Foundation the beneficiary of her policy, and provides them with instructions on how to dispense the proceeds of the policy. This could include a list of charities, and directions on the types of charities she'd like her money to go to, if any of the organizations no longer existed at the time of her death. Then on her passing, her estate gets one charitable receipt from the Foundation, and the job of dispersing her legacy gift rests in capable hands.

Sarah greatly appreciated this creative solution, and now regularly recommends her financial advisor to her friends and family members.

Chapter 9

STRUCTURING
THE IDEAL
CHARITABLE GIFT

"Think of giving not only as a duty,
but as a privilege."

— John D. Rockefeller,
American business magnate and philanthropist

Get the charity's name right

When you are directing a client on making a donation through their Will, or outside the estate using insurance, it is critical to ensure that directions on which organization receives the donation includes the full legal name of the organization, and to make the gift completely bulletproof, the organization's charitable registration number and mailing address. Battles over donations ensue when names are incomplete; for example, naming 'The Cancer Society' as the beneficiary of an insurance gift could cause cancer-related societies from across the world to line up for a chance of getting the gift. If there is no way to determine which was the intended recipient, the gift may not get to the charity, and tax relief for the gift will not come to the estate.

The legal name and registration numbers of charities are usually noted on the "Donate Now" page of their website. You can get this information from the *Canadian Donor's Guide to Fundraising Organizations in Canada* and/or *The Canadian Book of Charities – The Guide to Intelligent Giving* (for more information see *Chapter 10*). Alternately, the Canada Revenue Agency offers a webpage to search for any Canadian charity: http://bit.ly/1qPW3eL

Charitable registration numbers

Not all non-profits are registered charities. Some organizations whose primary role is advocacy (such as Greenpeace or Friends of Canadian Broadcasting) are not registered charities and therefore cannot offer charitable tax receipts. If your client is counting on receiving a charitable tax receipt to offset taxes, you may wish to search to see if their charity is indeed a registered Canadian charity.

Different ways to assign a charity to be beneficiary of an insurance donation

Depending on your client's circumstances, there are five ways that charities can be named as a beneficiary:

1. **Owner and Beneficiary** (life insurance). Benefits people who need tax relief during their lifetime. Because the donor grants ownership of a policy to a registered charity, the charity considers all of the premium payments made by the donor as charitable gifts. It will usually issue the donor one charitable tax receipt a year for the combined total of all premiums made over a calendar year. Charities learn the exact value of these payments by requesting confirmation from the insurance company each January. Donors do not receive charitable tax receipt for the death benefit that the charity receives when the donor dies.

2. **Beneficiary** (life insurance and all other insurance products). Can benefit those who will need charitable tax credits to offset estate taxes, people who wish to stay in control of their funds during their lifetime should their circumstances change, and people who like the idea that the gift they make is multiplied through the power of insurance. Because the donor can change a beneficiary at any time, the charity does not offer tax receipts for premiums, but only on the death benefit they receive when the donor dies.

3. **Irrevocable Beneficiary** (life insurance and all other insurance products). Used by people who want to ensure their charity receives the proceeds from an insurance policy or possible residue from insurance products. This does not mean that the beneficiary cannot be changed before the death of the policy owner; however, it can only be changed with the consent of the charity named as irrevocable beneficiary. Usually charities will not want to give up their beneficiary status. But if the charity is about to fulfill its mission and be terminated, it can permit the donor to change the beneficiary, perhaps to another charity with a similar mandate.

4. **Contingent Beneficiary** (life insurance and all other insurance products). Those who need insurance products to provide financial security for their family members can still possibly be philanthropic by naming a charity as a contingent beneficiary. The charity will receive the death benefit or product residue if the primary beneficiary is no longer alive when the policy owner dies. Naming a contingent beneficiary can also be wise to avoid the possibility that the organization they wish to support may no longer be around when the client dies. They can name a second charity as a contingent beneficiary to deal with this concern.

5. **Co-Beneficiary** (life insurance and all other insurance products). A donor can divide the proceeds from insurance products between more than one beneficiary. For example, a parent could name their children and a charity to be co-beneficiaries of one policy, or two or more charities can each receive a percentage. The policy owner decides what percentage each beneficiary receives.

What charities may or may not accept

All gifts of insurance are not equal in the eyes of charities. Insurance gifts can require manpower to manage, especially if a young donor assigns a charity to be an owner of life insurance.

Minimum life insurance policy sizes

Charities want to personally "steward" donors of any legacy gifts, but especially those who have made their charity a beneficiary of an insurance product, because at any time a donor can change his or her mind about the gift and change the beneficiary. Some charities may set a minimum gift amount they accept in a life insurance policy (often $5,000 - $10,000) because the money it costs them to steward a gift that may take decades to realize can outweigh the actual value of the donation. You or your client may wish to check with the fundraiser at the charity before making a gift of a small life insurance policy.

Donations of permanent life insurance policies

Many donors have the best intentions when buying a pay-for-life insurance policy and naming their charity as its owner and/or beneficiary. Donors feel like the premiums they pay are "donations" to the charity. But in reality, most people do not donate to the same charity for decades; their charitable giving priorities change over time with their interests and life experiences, and they move their charitable dollars from one organization to another. Charitable giving can also be affected by changes to a donor's health or financial circumstances. So it's important to know that gifts of life insurance that a donor pays for over his or her life tend to have a high failure rate because donors stop paying the premiums.

Sadly, when this happens, policies can lapse and become worthless. If the donor named the charity as its owner, the charity can look for another donor to pick up the premium payments, but more frequently, they will collapse the policy and claim the cash value that has accumulated. Because the failure rate has been high, you may find that some charities are not enthusiastic about receiving this kind of gift.

The back-to-back strategy, which marries annuities with a gift of life insurance (illustrated in *Chapter 1*), can also have the added benefit of lowering the overall premium payments of permanent policies as well as guaranteeing that the life policy will never lapse. Another option is for your client to back up a permanent life insurance policy donation by also making a gift of securities, accompanied by directions to apply the value of the security to paying future premiums.

Or you can direct your clients towards short pay life insurance policies that are guaranteed to be fully funded in 10 years or less. You will find that many people will like the idea of being able to give a lot more using life insurance and prefer to do so with only a short-term obligation.

Donations of life insurance policies that are no longer needed

There are times when people purchase life insurance for a specific reason (for example, a parent wants to provide for their child after the parent passes away) and then that reason ceases to exist (the child no longer requires financial support).

It is common that people offer unneeded policies to charities as gifts, since this is often the only kind of insurance gift that charities actively request. When the policies are fully paid up, requiring no more premiums to be paid to keep the policies in force, these gifts are welcomed by charities.

In return for donations of fully-funded policies, the charity will issue the donor a tax receipt for the policy's cash surrender value (CSV), or the fair market value (FMV), if that is greater. Although an in-force illustration reveals the CSV, FMV has to be determined by an actuary. In cases where the FMV can offer the donor a significantly larger tax receipt, you may find that the charity will ask the donor to cover the actuary's fee for this valuation (which can be about $2,000) by making a separate donation equal in size to the actuary's fee.

Charities are often put in a difficult position when people wish to transfer the ownership of partially paid short-term policies or T-100 policies to the organization, with the caveat that the charity continues to pay the premiums. Charities not-so-lovingly call these "Dump and Run" policy donations.

Most charities are unable to accept, manage or afford to take on the premiums of insurance policies, especially if the donor is healthy and may live on for decades. Those that do not have ongoing cash reserves to pay such premiums (despite the final amount that the policy may be worth) are forced to cash out these policies, and issue the donor a charitable tax receipt for the policy's cash CSV or FMV – whichever is greater. Donors often believe that they can get a tax receipt for the full death benefit, and express their disappointment to the charity, leaving bad feelings between the donor and charity. Some will withdraw their offer and shop their policy around to see if they can find a charity to pick up the premiums, so they can get a receipt for the full death benefit without realizing that the best they will get from a charity willing to take over premium payments is a receipt for the policy's FMV, as valued on the date of transfer of the policy's ownership to the charity.

If you learn that one of your clients is considering a donation of an insurance policy that is not fully funded, you should remind your client first that most charities do not have the cash to pay for premiums to keep such policies in force. However, a charity can still benefit from the gift, especially if it is a policy that has a level cost and is at least five years old – but it may need to collapse the policy for its cash surrender value after the transfer of ownership if your client no longer wishes to continue with the premium payments.

If your client continues the premium payments or the charity takes on the premium payments, the value of this gift will be typically worth Fair Market Value, as determined by an actuary – an amount determined by factors including the age of the insured, the value of premiums that have already been paid into the policy, its cash surrender value, and the policy's face value. You can point out that some charities ask the donor to make a cash donation to cover the actuary's fee (which can be around $2000). By informing your client in advance about this process, you can manage their expectations of the size of the gift and tax receipt from their transaction.

Donations of life insurance policies in which the charity is made co-owner with another charity or person

Co-owning a policy with another charity or person can be problematic for charities to administer, and may not be accepted.

Designated donations

It is not unusual that individuals like to make legacy gifts directed to the type of work done by their charity for which they have a special affinity. However, the work of charities often evolves over time, with certain programs or services changing or being eliminated to meet changing needs or funding challenges. If donors are too specific with their gift designation, it may be that the program they wish to support doesn't exist by the time their legacy gift is realized. You should always recommend that your clients contact the charity and discuss the intention of their gift to ensure they can make a gift that has a meaningful impact. The charity may wish to formalize donor wishes by having them sign a gift agreement.

Client likes the idea of giving using insurance, but is uninsurable

Age, illness or existing medical condition may either make your client uninsurable, or can make insurance excessively expensive. If this is the case and your client still likes the idea of the using the multiplying power of insurance to make a powerful gift, your client has the option of purchasing life insurance based on the life of a loved one (often a healthy spouse/partner or child), and assigning a charity as the policy's owner and beneficiary. To meet the rules of insurable interest on a policy based on the life of another, it must be deemed that the purchaser would suffer some kind of loss if the insured person died. The person insured has to formally register his or her consent to have a life insurance policy based on his or her life, on which a charity is owner and beneficiary. The funding of this kind of policy is often considered a loving gift made to the insured, especially when the charity being supported is also a favourite cause of the insured.

Chapter 10

LEARN MORE
AND BECOME CONNECTED

"How lovely to think that
no one need wait a moment;
we can start now,
start slowly changing the world."

— Anne Frank

Books and Online Resources

Bronfman, Charles & Jeffrey Solomon. (2012). *The Art of Doing Good – Where Passion Meets Action.* Jossey-Bass.

> An essential companion for anyone looking to start a non-profit organization with real impact. Features real-life stories of 18 notable social entrepreneurs and the organizations they run.

Bronfman, Charles & Jeffrey Solomon. (2009). *The Art of Giving – Where the Soul Meets a Business Plan.* Jossey-Bass.

> "There are thousands of books that teach us how to make money, but very few that teach us how to give effectively," said Charles Bronfman. "Giving is easy, but giving effectively and strategically requires both self-awareness and a solid business sense. Together with my co-author, our aim is to help accelerate a new generation of philanthropists along what can be a very steep learning curve."

Canada Helps
www.canadahelps.org/en/

For more information on Charitable Tax Credits
www.canadahelps.org/en/tag/tax/

Canadian Revenue Agency
www.cra-arc.gc.ca/chrts-gvng/menu-eng.html

> For information on charitable tax law, charitable tax receipts, an online search for any Canadian charity (including information their T3010 financial statements, and information on which can offer receipts and which cannot), and a donation tax credit calculator. The site includes a gallery of useful and easy-to-understands videos on several topics.

Canadian Donor's Guide to Fundraising Organizations in Canada, Third Sector Publishing.

An annual publication that includes articles on philanthropy, volunteering, tax considerations, charity standards, etc. Alphabetical, thematic and geographic list of Canadian charities, including legal name, address and charitable registration number.

Canadian Book of Charities, The – The Guide to Intelligent Giving. Mavor Publications.

An annual publication sent free to every law firm, corporation, trust company and granting agency in Canada. Includes only charities who pay for their listing.

Community Foundations of Canada
http://communityfoundations.ca/

CFC has a great online resource guide for professional advisors. It includes advice on talking with your clients about charitable giving, tools and resources on gift options and donor benefits, a charitable gift matrix to help you figure out the best charitable gift options for your client, and more information about how community foundations can enhance the services you offer to your clients. Includes a listing of Canadian Community Foundations, which offer Canadians advice and assistance on directing substantial gifts to charities.

Imagine Canada
www.imaginecanada.ca

Imagine Canada works alongside the charitable sector — often in partnership with the private sector, governments and individuals in the community — to ensure charities continue to play a pivotal role in building, enriching and defining our nation. They also offer a searchable resource called Charity

Focus that offers a profile of every charity in Canada:

www.imaginecanada.ca/resources-and-tools/charity-focus

Jamal, Azim & Harvey McKinnon. (2005). *The Power of Giving – Creating abundance in your home, at work, and in your community.* Jeremy P. Tarcher/Penguin.

Minton, Frank & Lorna Somers.(1998). *Planned Giving for Canadians.* Somersmith.

> Primarily a guide for those in the non-profit sector and registered charities this is a great overview for anyone interested in a deeper understanding of the workings of charities. Chapter 5 provides a comprehensive guide for donors and their advisors on various effective ways to give.

Pallotta, Dan. (2008). *Uncharitable – How Restraints on Nonprofits Undermine their Potential.* Tufts University Press.

> Most of your clients will want to evaluate whether they should support a charity or not based on the cost of their administration expenses, how much the staff are paid, and how much is spent on fundraising. In a groundbreaking must-read book, Dan Pallotta argues that this Puritan ethic deprives nonprofits of tools and permissions freely used by the for-profit sector, which hobbles nonprofits from being able to effectively achieve their goals.
> For a taste of what this book is about, listen to Dan Pallotta's TedTalk: http://bit.ly/1ooDyJI

Solie, David. (2004) *How to Say It to Seniors – Closing the Communications Gap with our Elders*, Penguin.

Turcotte, Martin. (2012) *Charitable Giving by Canadians*, Statistics Canada.

> On average, 84% of Canadians 15 and older — or just under

24 million people — reported making at least one financial donation to a charitable or nonprofit organization. This number climbs to 94% if you include gifts of material goods or food. This Statistics Canada study released in 2012 details who constitutes a typical Canadian donor and what motivates them to give. http://bit.ly/1RgXQFe

Get Connected

Bequest Insurance
www.bequestinsurance.ca

Canada's experts on using life insurance and insurance products to multiply charitable giving, meet life's goals and disinherit the taxman. Co-founded by Judy Doré, a Burlington, Ontario based financial advisor and insurance expert; Jack Bergmans, of Toronto, Ontario, Certified Financial Planner and insurance expert; and Marlena McCarthy, fundraising and marketing expert. Marlena and Jack have authored the books *Ripple Effect: Growing your business with insurance and philanthropy* and *Multiplying Generosity: Creatively using insurance to increase legacy gifts.*

Canadian Association of Gift Planners (CAGP)
www.cagp-acpdp.org

All of the staff at Bequest Insurance are members of the Canadian Association of Gift Planners, whose vision is to inspire giving through enlightened planning, and whose mission is to advance gift planning in Canada. CAGP welcomes as its members professional advisors (financial advisors, lawyers, accountants) and fundraisers. There are chapters across Canada, and most have periodic lunch-and-learn or breakfast meetings with a knowledgeable guest speaker. The organization also holds an annual conference, alternating each year from a location in eastern Canada to a western location. Attending CAGP events helps financial advisors better understand trends in charitable giving, charity and tax law, and the challenges that Canadian charities face when asking for and receiving bequests made in a myriad of ways. Presentations are interactive and solution-oriented. They are a great way to learn and remain current about legacy giving, to increase your value as an advisor.

Canadian Revenue Agency
www.cra-arc.gc.ca/chrts-gvng/menu-eng.html

For information on charitable tax law, charitable tax receipts, an online search for any Canadian charity (including information their T3010 financial statements, and information on which can offer receipts and which cannot), and a donation tax credit calculator. The site includes a gallery of useful and easy-to-understands videos on several topics.

Miller Thomson, experts in Canadian tax law
www.millerthomson.com

Law offices across Canada; lawyers have particular expertise in charitable law. Their monthly online *Charities and Not-for-Profit Newsletter* offers careful analysis of the ever-changing Canadian charitable tax landscape. http://bit.ly/1f7n86Q

Mind*path*™
www.mindpath.ca

Mind*path* is a Canadian educational conference company for financial industry advisors, run by financial advisors. It has annual *Doing Well by Doing Good – Growing Your Financial Advisory Practice through Philanthropy* day-long conferences, usually held in the Greater Toronto area, Ottawa, or Vancouver. Well-chosen speakers include financial advisors who successfully incorporate philanthropy into their practices, and fundraisers from top

Canadian charities. There are also Continuing Education Credits offered for some of the presentations at these conferences.

Bequest Insurance has spoken on different aspects of giving using insurance, and regularly attends the conferences as a participant. We highly recommend attending these targeted events.

APPENDIX

Sample document providing instructions on insurance donations to leave with Will for Executor

TO THE EXECUTOR OF <ENTER NAME>'S ESTATE

I, <*Enter full legal name*>, have left the following donation(s) of life insurance or insurance products to charity:

a. **Life insurance policy**, Policy number XXXXX, with <*Name of Insurance Company*>. On this policy, I have named <*legal name of charity*> as the owner and beneficiary / beneficiary / irrevocable beneficiary/co-beneficiary/ contingent beneficiary in the case that <*Name of primary beneficiary*> has predeceased me. Please contact the above noted insurance company and forward them a copy of my death certificate, to expedite my charity receiving the death benefit from this insurance policy. [To add if the charity has been named **owner** of the policy:] Please anticipate that the aforementioned charity will send to my estate a charitable tax receipt for the full value of the death benefit they will receive, which can be applied against 100% of my final year's net income. If the tax credit is larger than the taxes owing on the final return, the balance of the tax credit can be against 100% of my net income in the year before my death to reclaim taxes submitted in that year.

b. **Annuity <or Variable Annuity / Segregated Fund / GIC / RRSP / RRIF / any other insurance product held in an insurance company>**, Contract number XXXXX, with <*Name of Insurance Company*>. I have named <*legal name of charity*> as the <owner and beneficiary / beneficiary / irrevocable beneficiary/co-beneficiary/contingent beneficiary> of the aforementioned insurance product. The beneficiary should receive any residue remaining as of the date of my death. Please contact the above noted insurance company and if there are any residual funds left, forward the insurance company a copy of my death certificate. Anticipate that the aforementioned charity will send to my estate a charitable tax receipt for any residual funds that it will receive, which should be applied against 100% of my final year's net income. If the tax credit is larger than the taxes owing on the final return, the balance of the tax credit should be used against 100% of my net income in the year before my death to reclaim taxes submitted in that year.

1. Statements and other documentation of this life insurance policy / insurance products can be found in *<location of insurance paperwork>*.

2. I have made the charity aware that they will be receiving this gift.
   or
   I have not made the charity aware that they will be receiving this gift.

3. I have made my family / loved ones aware of this gift.
   or
   I have purposely not shared information about this gift with my family, loved ones or friends. I wish to keep this gift private. Please do not let them know I have made this gift.
   or
   During my lifetime, I have purposely not shared information about this gift with my family, loved ones or friends. After my death, and after my charity has received the gift (*after one month of the insurance company receiving my death certificate from you*), please share information about this donation with *<Names of specific individuals>*.

Signature: _____

Date: _____

Printed name of Signer: _____

To download a Word version of this form, go to www.bequestinsurance. ca/Executor_Form.php

ABBREVIATIONS

CAGP Canadian Association of Gift Planners

CPP   Canada Pension Plan

CRA   Canada Revenue Agency

CSV   Cash Surrender Value

DAF   Donor Advised Fund

FMV   Fair Market Value

GIA   Guaranteed Investment Account

GIC   Guaranteed Investment Certificate

GIS   Guaranteed Income Supplement

GMWB Guaranteed Minimum Withdrawal Benefit

LIF   Life Income Fund

LIRA   Locked-in Retired Account

LRIF   Locked-in Retirement Income Fund

OAS   Old Age Security

RRIF   Registered Retirement Income Fund

RRSP   Registered Retirement Savings Plan

TFSA   Tax-Free Savings Account

GLOSSARY

Not all of these words or concepts are used in this book, but may take some of the mystery out of conversations you will have with financial advisors, lawyers or accountants.

Accumulation annuity
See guaranteed interest account.

Actuary
A business professional qualified to mathematically calculate commercial and financial risks and probabilities on uncertain future events, based on statistics and laws of averages. Actuaries are used by insurance companies to calculate insurance premiums, and by charities to determine the fair market value of life insurance policies, for tax receipting purposes.

Adjustable life insurance
A permanent life insurance policy whose premiums get less expensive when interest rates rise, and more expensive when interest rates drop.

Agent
See insurance agent.

Annual renewal term insurance
See year renewal term insurance.

Annuitant

1. A person who receives the benefits of an annuity or pension. An annuity contract can have more than one annuitant.

2. A person upon whom a life insurance contract is based.

Annuity
A series of income payments or receipts made at yearly or at

other regular intervals for life or specific period of time or term.

Annuity contract
A contractual agreement with a life insurance company that will provide regular payments for life or at regular intervals in exchange for a lump sum payment. The owner of the annuity contract may or may not be the annuitant.

Assuris
A not-for-profit organization that protects Canadian insurance policyholders if their life insurance company fails. It minimizes the loss of benefits and ensures a quick transfer of policies to a solvent company, where their protected benefits will continue. Assuris guarantees policyholders will retain 100% of the values up to certain maximum thresholds and after that at least 85% of the insurance benefits they are promised, including death, health expense, monthly income and cash value. For deposit-type products like *guaranteed investment certificates*, Assuris guarantees the owner will retain 100% of their accumulated value up only to $100,000, just like the Canada Deposit Insurance Corporation coverage found in banks and trust companies.

Back-to-back strategy
Also known as insured annuities. When an individual guarantees that a gifted insurance policy with life-long premium payments does not lapse by purchasing an annuity whose life-long payments are used to pay their insurance premiums.

Beneficiary
The individual or organization that receives life insurance proceeds or the residue remaining in insured investment products upon the death of the insured. All insurance products and investments allow the owner to assign a beneficiary to receive the policy's death benefit, or any residual amount left in annuities or other investments on the insured/owner's death.

Multiple beneficiaries are allowed. They can include individuals, businesses/organizations and charities.

Cash value/Cash surrender value
The cash an insurance company will pay to the insurance policy owner if his or her policy is voluntarily terminated before its maturity or before the death of the person insured. This cash value is the savings component of most permanent (not term) life insurance policies. When cashing out a policy, the insurance company first deducts any withdrawn interest and loans taken out by the owner against the policy to determine its current net cash value.

Certificate of deposit
See guaranteed investment certificate.

Charitable gift annuities
Also known as gift plus annuities or reinsured charitable gift annuities. A donation strategy offered to donors directly by certain charities. Popular with retirees who want to receive regular, guaranteed income for life, while also making a significant charitable gift. The donor makes an upfront payment for their annuity to the charity, which retains a minimum of 20 percent as a charitable gift, which is receipted immediately. The charity then funds an annuity with the balance of the funds, and directs the annuity payments to the donor.

Co-beneficiary
When a person assigns more than one beneficiary to their insurance policies, annuities or insurance investment products, beneficiaries are referred to as co-beneficiaries.

Community foundation
Non-profit organizations that help Canadians invest in building strong and resilient places to live, work and play. They can be employed to help facilitate charitable gifts. In Canada, community foundations can be identified through Community

Foundations of Canada (http://communityfoundations.ca/).

Commuted value
The present value of the future payments at a point in time of an annuity.

Commuting
Converting an annuity to its equivalent lump sum value.

Contingent beneficiary
Any insurance product can be assigned one or more back-up or contingent beneficiaries – people or organizations who will receive funds from insurance products if the primary beneficiary(ies) predecease the insured, or in the case of an charitable beneficiary, the charity ceases to exist before the death of the donor.

Contract
Term used by insurance agents/brokers to describe any insurance product purchased by a client.

Death benefit
The amount payable to a beneficiary(ies) of a life insurance policy or insurance product such as a GIC, segregated fund or annuity, after the insured person has died. If there is more than one beneficiary, each beneficiary gets whatever portion of the death benefit that was specified by the owner of the insurance contract. Beneficiaries cannot be changed by anyone other than the contract owner, not even by the owner's power of attorney. Death benefits can be a fixed (*or level*) amount as defined in the insurance contract, or can increase or decrease over time.

Deferred annuity
A term or life annuity contract in which the payments do not commence until a specific date that may be based upon the annuitant's age. The premium for the deferred annuity can be funded with a lump sum or through periodic payments.

Dependent
A person who relies on another for support or their primary source of income. Examples can include spouse, minor child, infirm child over 18.

Disbursement quota
The minimum legally defined amount a Canadian registered charity is obliged to spend each year on its charitable activities or on gifts to qualified donees (e.g. other registered charities). The disbursement quota (DQ) is based on the value of the charity's property not used for charitable activities or administration. Income received from gifts of life insurance is not considered fundraised income, and is not considered when calculating the DQ. Also, *unmatured life insurance policies* are not considered a charitable asset and are not counted when calculating the DQ.

Face amount / Face value
The amount of insurance coverage purchased by the policyholder.

Fair market value
A complicated calculation done by an actuary on a life insurance policy to determine its value at the time of the evaluation, following guidelines in the Canadian Revenue Agency's Information Circular IC-89-3. This amount is often larger than a policy's cash surrender value and less than its death benefit. The fee for an actuary to perform a fair market value on a policy can be in the $2,000 range.

Fixed annuity
An insurance contract in which the insurance company contractually guarantees payments to the annuitant for the term of the contract in exchange for a lump sum.

Fully-funded policy
Also known as a paid-up policy. A life insurance policy that has

accumulated sufficient cash value to cover the cost of all future premiums, without further payments from the insured.

Gift plus annuities
See charitable gift annuities.

Graded premiums
Policies with premiums that increase incrementally for a certain number of years, and thereafter remain level. Attractive to younger people who anticipate growth in future earnings.

Guaranteed interest account (GIA)
Also known as a guaranteed investment account or an accumulation annuity. Valued as a low-risk investment, the GIA is a deposit-type investment product offered by insurance companies, similar to GICs found at banks. Deposits into GIAs are accumulated for the purpose of providing a guaranteed lump sum in the future. When a GIA matures, the owner has the option of rolling the lump sum (principal plus accrued interest) into an annuity, or receiving the cash surrender value. GIAs offer holding periods of one to five years or more at guaranteed interest rates. Additional benefits include the residual value passing to named beneficiary(ies) outside of the estate to ease the transfer of wealth, possible creditor protection, and a guaranteed death benefit that includes the principal and all accrued interest.

Guaranteed investment certificate
Also known as GICs, certificate of deposit, time deposit or term deposit. Investment vehicles, sold by banks, trust companies and credit unions, which offer a guaranteed rate of return over a 1 to 5 year period. Valued as a low-risk investment.

Guaranteed minimum withdrawal benefit (GMWB)
An annuity with contractually guaranteed minimum payments for life or a given period. Payments may rise over time, depending on the performance of underlying investments.

Guaranteed premium return annuity

A *life annuity* that includes a guarantee that at least the full amount of the initial investment or premium payment will be paid out.

Immediate annuity

Usually refers to an annuity whose first payment is one month after the annuity is purchased, although by strict definition the first payment could take place within one year of purchase.

Increasing term insurance

See year renewal term insurance.

Indexed annuity

An annuity that includes a provision for increased payments over time, normally as a hedge against inflation.

In-force

An adjective used by insurance professionals that describes an active insurance policy.

In-force illustration

Details supplied by an insurance company on the current and future status and value of a life insurance policy as it stands at that time. The illustration includes the face value of the policy, cost of premium payments, accumulated cash value, the change in size of the policy over time (if any), and the death benefit. It will also indicate if the policy will lapse, and how much needs to be added to keep the policy from lapsing. Also, an in-force illustration can be requested to project certain assumptions for the future on an existing policy – for example, what would happen to a policy's death benefit if the policy's premiums are increased or decreased by a certain amount.

Insurability

The conditions on a life insurance applicant that are required by the life insurance company. To determine whether to issue a policy and the amount of premium to charge, an insurance company conducts an underwriting process that takes into consideration such things as the health and financial situation of the insured, their age, whether they smoke or not, their weight and occupation, and the amount of life insurance already in force on the life of that person.

Insurance agent
Insurance agents help clients choose insurance policies that suit their needs. Clients include individuals, families and businesses. Captive agents work for and only sell a single insurance company's products or specified products of other insurance companies. Independent insurance agents (*or brokers*), represent several companies. Agents must usually be licensed within the province or territory in which they do business.

Insurable interest
To prevent mischief and/or speculation on the death of persons unconnected to a life insurance policy buyer, a life insurance policy can be purchased only by those who would suffer some kind of loss if the insured dies. They are said to have an "insurable interest." In the case of a charity owning a policy based on the life of a donor, the charity does not have an insurable interest on the donor, but all that is required to validate the donation of a life insurance policy is the donor's written consent noted on the beneficiary section of an insurance application or on a beneficiary change form – a minor formality.

Insurance broker
An insurance broker (also insurance agent) qualified to sell, solicit and negotiate insurance in the province or territory in which they are licensed. Canadian brokers must be licensed by each province or territory in which they do business.

Insured (The)
Also see *insurable interest*. The individual on whose life an insurance policy is based. Policy proceeds are paid upon the

death of the insured. The owner and the insured are often the same person, but they need not be the same.

Insured annuities
See back-to-back strategy.

Insurer
Insurance company that issues the insurance policy.

Irrevocable beneficiary
When the beneficiary status of a life insurance policy, annuity or any other insurance product is made irrevocable, it can only be changed with the permission of the named beneficiary. The irrevocable beneficiary also has to agree to adding other beneficiaries, or to surrendering (or collapsing) the policy before the death of the owner for the purpose of collecting the cash surrender value. However, the policy owner can still let such a policy lapse by not paying premiums, unless ordered by the court to continue paying the premiums.

Joint and last survivor annuity
A pension that is payable to two annuitants, and that includes a provision that payments continue for the life of the survivor after the first annuitant dies.

Joint last-to-die life insurance policy
Life insurance policies based on insuring two lives (a couple, siblings or close friends). The policy remains in force when the first of the two insured persons die; the death benefit only goes to the beneficiary after the death of the second insured person.

Level cost of insurance
Life insurance premiums that remain the same over the life of an insurance contract.

Life annuity
An annuity where payments are guaranteed for the life of the annuitant(s).

Life annuity with a guaranteed term
A life annuity that includes a clause that guarantees that payments will continue for a specific period, even if the annuitant dies before the guaranteed period expires. If the annuitant dies before the term, the guaranteed payments can be continued to beneficiaries as 'successor annuitants' for the duration of the contract or beneficiaries may receive a lump sum.

Life income fund (LIF)
A registered retirement income fund into which funds previously held in pension funds have been transferred. There are annual minimum and maximum amounts that can be withdrawn from the plan, as specified by the Income Tax Act. A LIF can be converted to a life annuity.

Life pay insurance
For more, see T-100 life insurance. Life insurance policies that require premiums to be paid until the insured dies.

Limited pay life insurance
See short-pay life insurance.

Locked-in retirement account (LIRA)
Also known as a locked-in retirement income fund (LRIF) in British Columbia, Nova Scotia, PEI, Yukon, NW Territories and by the Federal government. A registered retirement savings plan into which funds previously held in pension funds have been transferred and are held until the legal age of retirement, when the owner is required to begin extracting income. At that point the LIRA or LRIF is converted to a life income fund (LIF).

Locked-in retirement income fund (LRIF)
Also known as a locked-in RRIF. A retirement fund that receives funds from a locked-in retirement account and provides retirement income by that is limited by minimum and maximum withdrawal amounts.

Locked-in RRIF (LRIF)
See locked-in retirement income fund.

Locked-in RRSP (LRSP)
See locked-in retirement account.

Medical examination
Part of the insurance underwriting process, to determine whether an individual is insurable. Depending on the type and size of insurance policy, an applicant may have to either answer a written questionnaire about their health, have blood or urine taken by a nurse sent from a company that specifically completes medical examinations for insurance companies, or may require a more thorough exam or documentation from the applicant's family doctor.

Minimum amount
The amount that must be withdrawn from a RRIF each year, beginning the year after the RRIF is established, in accordance with the Income Tax Act – ITA 146.3(1).

Modified premium life insurance
Policies with premiums that remain fixed at a relatively low level for a certain number of years, then increase substantially in a single year to the level where they remain. Attractive option for younger people who anticipate growth in future earnings.

Net present value calculation
Also known as net present worth. A mathematical calculation to estimate the current value of an insurance policy (or other financial investments).

Normal annuity
An annuity that for income tax purposes calculate the interest and principal according to an amortization schedule, whereby early payments consist of a higher proportion of interest than later payments.

Old Age Security Program (OAS)
A monthly payment available to most Canadians 65 years of age and older who meet the Canadian legal status and residence requirements. Source: Old Age Security Pension, Service Canada. http://bit.ly/1GGGGRc

Owner
The individual or entity that owns a life insurance policy (also known as "the insurance contract"). The owner is usually the insured, and is responsible for paying premiums. In the case of policies purchased by donors who have assigned charities to be their owners, the donor who is insured is responsible for making the premium payments. If the donor has to stop making payments, the charity can continue making the payments, or collapse the policy and extract whatever net cash value has been accumulated.

Paid-up policy
See fully-funded policy.

Participating life insurance policies
Typically, these are life insurance contracts with a growing death benefit such as a whole life participating policies. Premiums paid on the policies are invested, which creates a growing cash value that is annually added to the policy as a dividend. The dividend can be relatively generous but is usually not contractually guaranteed. The dividend can be used different ways by the policy holder; e.g. to pay the insurance policy's premium payment or withdrawn for immediate use. Or, the dividend can be kept within the insurance contract as a deposit to generate interest much like a savings account at a bank.

Permanent life insurance
Life insurance policies where a death benefit is guaranteed when the insured passes away (provided the policy is in-force). T-100, whole life and universal life policies are examples of permanent insurance.

Policy
A legal contract between an individual or company and an insurance company (the insurer). Policies specify what risks are covered by the insurer; under what circumstances the insurer will pay the policy beneficiaries; how much money or type of benefit the insured will receive upon death or if the insured makes a claim; and who will be the beneficiary(ies) of the policy.

Premium offset
The cash value of a policy which pays the premiums (cost of insurance) until the cash value is completely depleted. In some cases, policies can accumulate enough cash value to pay the cost of insurance for the remainder of the insured's life.

Premiums
Payments made on life insurance policies.

Prescribed annuity
Provides payments that have a level interest component throughout the life of the contract. Available only for non-registered plans are very attractive for those seeking higher income through lower income taxes.

Probate
The legal procedure to validate a Will, formally confirm the appointment of the executor, and pay estate taxes. Officially known in Ontario as "Certificate of Appointment of Estate Trustee With a Will" or "Certificate of Appointment of Estate Trustee Without a Will". Probate taxes and related fees vary depending on where in Canada the deceased lived, and the value of his or her estate's assets. Typically a lawyer is employed to file and process a probate application on behalf of the executor. There may also be accountant's fees to prepare the application. These additional fees may be for time spent on an hourly basis, or on a percentage of the size of the estate, or both.

Quick pay life insurance policies
See short-pay life insurance.

Registered annuity
An annuity purchased from an insurance company with transferred registered savings, like Registered Retirement Savings Plans (RRSPs), Locked-in Retirement Account funds (LIRA) or Registered Retirement Income Funds (RRIFs).

Registered funds
Also known as tax-deferred savings. Savings held within registered plans. These include: Registered Retirement Savings Plans (RRSPs), Registered Retirement Income Funds (RRIFs), Locked-in Retirement Account funds (LRIFs), and Locked-in Retirement Accounts (LIRAs). When these are donated to charity, their entire value goes to the charity; the charitable tax receipt received will help to offset the income taxes owing on these accounts. In Ontario, Canada, probate taxes on registered accounts are waived if the entire residual amount is donated to a registered charity and/or other named beneficiaries.

Registered Retirement Income Fund (RRIF)
A Registered Retirement Income Fund (RRIF) is a tax-deferred retirement plan under Canadian tax law. Individuals use an RRIF to generate income from the savings accumulated under their Registered Retirement Savings Plan (RRSP). As with an RRSP, an RRIF account is registered with the Canada Revenue Agency. Individuals must convert an RRSP/LIRA to an income product, such as a RRIF, LRIF, or an annuity by December 31st in the year they turn 71. Income received from a RRIF is taxed at the highest rate as regular income.

Registered Retirement Savings Plan (RRSP)
A legal trust registered with the Canada Revenue Agency that is used by individuals to save for retirement. RRSP contributions are tax deductible and funds in RRSP accounts are deferred until the money is withdrawn. Money withdrawn

from a RRSP is tax deferred until the money is withdrawn.

Reinsured charitable gift annuities
See charitable gift annuities.

Segregated funds
Investment funds offered by insurance companies. They combine characteristics of the income and growth potential of a mutual fund. They add the security of capital guarantees, and many of the tax and estate benefits of a life insurance policy Segregated funds are invested in a managed pool of selected stocks, bonds, debentures and even other funds. Many estates can benefit from tax relief and increased income to heirs if charities are named as beneficiaries of these funds.

Short-pay policies
Also known as quick-pay or limited pay policies. Life insurance policies that can be fully funded and self-sustaining within a pre-determined period of time, or with a single payment.

Single life annuity
An annuity where payments are guaranteed for the life of a single annuitant.

Single pay life insurance policy
A policy that can be fully funded with one payment.

Specified death benefit
A predetermined fixed value to be received by beneficiaries of a life insurance policy.

Split-value life insurance policy
Also known as co-beneficiaries. When there are two or more beneficiaries assigned to a life insurance policy.

Spousal Registered Retirement Income Fund
Any RRIF created from a spousal or common-law Registered Retirement Savings Plan.

Spousal (or common-law) Registered Retirement Savings Plan
Intended as an effective way for couples to split taxable income
at retirement. An RRSP funded by a person (usually the higher
income earning spouse), up to their own annual RRSP limit,
for the benefit of their spouse or common-law partner to
receive income. The contributing spouse claims the annual tax
deductions on the contributions they make into the spousal
RRSP.

Straight-life annuity
An insurance contract that provides nothing more than
periodic payments to an annuitant until his or her death.

Successor annuitant
An option offered by most insurance contracts. A successor
annuitant receives continued payments after the death of the
original annuitant. For example, an owner and annuitant of a
RRIF may elect to have RRIF payments continue to go to his
spouse or common-law partner after his death.

T-100 life insurance
Permanent insurance policies that require a policy holder to
pay either monthly or annual premiums for the rest of his or
her life, or to age 100, whichever comes first. These policies do
not offer the owner the option of making additional payments
above the cost of insurance to produce a cash value that will
pay future premium payments. It would be extremely rare that
a T-100 would have a cash value.

Term certain annuity
A contract for the annuitant to receive regular and periodic
payments for a specified period of time or term. Includes a
guarantee that the payments will be made for the full term,
even if the annuitant dies before the term expires.

Term deposit
See guaranteed investment certificate.

Term insurance

Insurance provided for a specific time period and which pays a death benefit if the insured dies within that period. Often, no cash value accumulates in these policies. The death benefit may not change while the policy is in force, or benefits may decrease in tandem with a decreased obligation insured by the policy. Often used as a cheap substitute for mortgage insurance. If the policy owner does not die during the policy's term, the policy is collapsed and becomes valueless, with the exception of Term 100 insurance, which is a form of permanent insurance. Most insurance companies allow term insurance to be converted into a permanent insurance policy, which may become a charitable gift opportunity.

Underwriting

Insurance companies study the risk they take on by insuring life insurance applicants through an underwriting process. Underwriters look at such things as how much in-force insurance applicants own, and calculate risk based on applicants' health, weight, gender, age, whether they smoke, and sometimes their occupation. After completion of a medical history questionnaire and/or a simple or more complex medical examination, underwriters decide how much coverage an individual can receive, what the insurance premium payments will be, or whether applicants are too high risk and therefore uninsurable. By measuring these risks, underwriters work to protect the long-term viability of their insurance company, and its ability to meet all its obligations to its clients.

Universal life insurance

Universal life policies are a type of permanent insurance in which the premiums are invested and generate a growing tax-free cash value. These are often ideal for donors who want to make a donation of an insurance policy that becomes fully funded and self-sustaining. Over the payment period (which can be as little as one payment or can be set for a certain number of years or life), universal policies can accumulate sufficient cash value to pay all future premiums. As charitable donations, policies that are expected to be guaranteed to be self-funding, and that also guarantee a minimum death benefit are usually the best fit. This product can be used for *short-pay policies*.

Unmatured life insurance policies
Life insurance policies that are still in effect either because the person on whose life the policy is insured is still alive, or the term on the policy has not yet expired.

Unregistered annuity
An annuity purchased with unregistered funds.

Variable annuity
An insurance investment product often used for retirement income. Similar to an annuity, it offers guaranteed minimum payments and client access to the investments at any time. The funds placed in the variable annuities are invested in a managed portfolio; if investment performance exceeds a contractually guaranteed minimum amount, the payments will also increase in size. Billions of Canadian dollars are invested in variable annuities. Charities can be assigned as a successor annuitant to receive residual income or as a beneficiary to receive a lump sum from the remaining value upon the death of the owner.

Whole life insurance
A whole life policy provides a guaranteed death benefit plus any cash value that has accumulated in the policy over the lifetime of the insured. Some whole life policies pay dividends, which can pay future premiums, received in cash, used as collateral for loans, or used to purchase paid-up additional nsurance. There is also an option for an owner to use the accumulated dividends to self-fund the policy, which may result in a lower death benefit – *see reduced paid-up life insurance policy*.

Year renewal term insurance

(*Also known as YRT; increasing term insurance; annual renewal term insurance*). One-year term life insurance policy with premiums based on the owner's age and other risk factors. Premiums increase in every subsequent year that the policy is renewed. Especially attractive to younger people because of its initial low premiums and the payment of a death benefit to named beneficiaries if the policyholder passes away within the year term of the contract, but annual renewal and increasing premiums often lead to policies eventually being terminated.

ABOUT THE AUTHORS

Jack Bergmans

As a founding partner of Bequest Insurance, Jack is one of Canada's leading experts in integrating insurance into financial, estate and legacy planning. Jack is a Certified Financial Planner and has been in the investment industry since 1996. As a licensed insurance broker, he works with individuals and organizations providing independent financial, investment and retirement advice, and is also an estate planning and legacy giving specialist. Jack has previously worked in various financial planning roles with Manulife Financial, BMO Nesbitt Burns and Altamira Financial Services. Jack can also be found on a golf course, tennis court or bowling alley, and putting his creative culinary talents to good use cooking for his wife Marlena McCarthy and their friends.

Marlena McCarthy

Marlena McCarthy has worked with charities since 1982 in marketing, communications and fundraising. As Founding Partner and Fundraising and Communications Director of Bequest Insurance (www.bequestinsurance.ca), Marlena works with charities to help create income streams from gifts of life insurance and insurance products by creating simple yet gripping promotional materials. Through her Done Write Communications business (www.donewrite.com), Marlena acts as a fundraising consultant and writer for non-profits, specializing in planned giving promotion, direct mail fundraising, mid-level donor programs, and donor communications materials. In her spare time, she loves singing with her a cappella quartet Spadina Station, and chumming around with her husband, Jack Bergmans.